SAM HOLCROFT

Sam Holcroft's other plays include *The Wardrobe,* for National Theatre Connections, and *Edgar & Annabel*, part of the *Double Feature* season in the Paintframe at the National Theatre; *Dancing Bears*, part of the *Charged* season for Clean Break at Soho Theatre and Latitude Festival; *While You Lie* at the Traverse, Edinburgh; *Pink*, part of the *Women, Power and Politics* season at the Tricycle; *Vanya*, adapted from Chekhov, at The Gate; and *Cockroach*, co-produced by the National Theatre of Scotland and the Traverse (nominated for Best New Play 2008, by the Critics' Awards for Theatre in Scotland and shortlisted for the John Whiting Award, 2009). In 2013, Sam wrote *The House Taken Over*, a libretto for opera, adapted from Cortázar, for the Festival d'Aix-en-Provence and Académie Européenne de Musique. Sam received the Tom Erhardt Award in 2009, was the Pearson Writer-in-Residence at the Traverse Theatre, 2009–10, and the Writer-in-Residence at the National Theatre Studio from 2013–14. In 2014, Sam received a Windham Campbell Prize for Literature in the drama category.

Other Titles in this Series

Sam Holcroft

RULES FOR LIVING

NICK HERN BOOKS

London

www.nickhernbooks.co.uk

A Nick Hern Book

Rules for Living first published as a paperback orginal in Great Britain in 2015 by Nick Hern Books Limited, The Glasshouse, 49a Goldhawk Road, London W12 8QP

Reprinted with revisions 2016

Rules for Living copyright © 2015, 2016 Sam Holcroft

Sam Holcroft has asserted her right to be identified as the author of this work

Cover illustration by Tobatron

Designed and typeset by Nick Hern Books, London
Printed in Great Britain by CPI Group (UK) Ltd

A CIP catalogue record for this book is available from the British Library

ISBN   978 1 84842 469 2

Rules for Living was first performed in the Dorfman auditorium at the National Theatre, London, on 13 March 2015, with the following cast:

MATTHEW	Miles Jupp
CARRIE	Maggie Service
SHEENA	Claudie Blakley
ADAM	Stephen Mangan
EDITH	Deborah Findlay
FRANCIS	John Rogan
EMMA	Daisy Waterstone

Director	Marianne Elliott
Designer	Chloe Lamford
Lighting Designer	Neil Austin
Music	Adrian Sutton
Sound Designer	Ian Dickinson
Fight Director	Kate Waters
Company Voice Work	Jeannette Nelson
Staff Director	Melanie Spencer

Acknowledgements

Special thanks to Paul Lamond Games, creators and manufacturers of the fantastic card game Bedlam. In a play about constantly changing rules this game seemed the perfect complement.

Special thanks to Melanie Fennell, writer of *Overcoming Low Self-Esteem – a self-help guide using cognitive behavioral techniques*. Both the title of the play (*Rules for Living*) and its central conceit (characters obeying various 'rules' based out of their insecurities) were inspired by this brilliant book.

Thanks to all those who helped to develop the play in workshops including Mark Rose, Helen Schlesinger, John Heffernan, Deborah Findlay, Dan Skinner, Maggie Service, Miles Jupp, Nick Sidi and Lucy Robinson. And thanks to those directors who played Bedlam with me for hours: Amy Hodge, Daniel Bailey, Tim Hoare, Hannah Mulder, Tom Hughes and Bryony Shanahan.

Thanks to all at the National Theatre Studio.

Thanks to the cast, crew and design team.

Thanks to Nick Hytner, Sebastian Born and Ben Power.

Thanks to Mel Kenyon and Lydia Rynne.

Thanks to my family.

Enormous thanks to Marianne Elliott.

And lastly, but most importantly, thanks to Ali. My hero.

S.H.

Characters

MATTHEW, *thirties, boyfriend of Carrie*
CARRIE, *thirties, girlfriend of Matthew*
SHEENA, *forties, married to Adam*
ADAM, *forties, married to Sheena*
EDITH, *sixties, married to Francis, mother to Adam and Matthew*
FRANCIS, *seventies, married to Edith, father to Adam and Matthew*
EMMA, *fourteen, daughter of Adam and Sheena*

Setting

The entire play is set in an open-plan kitchen/living room, or kitchen-conservatory of a family home on Christmas Day.

There are three entrances: one to the garden, one leading to the rest of the house, and one opening onto a utility room/larder.

Notes on the Rules

The rules are cumulative: once they appear, each rule applies throughout the rest of the play.

The rules will work best if integrated into organic actions – characters finding naturalistic reasons to sit, stand, etc.

The rules give both 'necessary and sufficient' conditions to the characters. By which I mean: when a rule states that 'Matthew must sit to tell a lie,' this means *both* that 'when Matthew is sitting, he is always lying', *and* that 'when Matthew is lying, he is always sitting.' The audience will gradually learn this from watching the play unfold. I decided not to clutter the rules by attempting to express it directly ('Matthew may sit *if and only if* he is lying…').

ACT ONE

Scene One

25th December, mid-morning.

An open-plan kitchen/living room or kitchen-conservatory of a large family home.

CARRIE and MATTHEW, an unmarried couple in their thirties, unpack their contributions onto the kitchen table: food, alcohol, presents.

MATTHEW. Carrie… are you okay?

CARRIE. What?

MATTHEW. Are you okay?

CARRIE. Am I okay?

MATTHEW. Yes.

CARRIE. Yes, of course I'm okay. I'm fine.

MATTHEW. Honey, I know that face – what's wrong?

CARRIE. Shush.

MATTHEW. Sheena can't hear us.

CARRIE. Would you keep your voice down?

MATTHEW. She's two floors up; she can't hear us. (*Calling.*) Sheena?

CARRIE. Matthew.

MATTHEW (*calling louder*). Sheena?

There is no response.

See? I grew up in this house – I know what you can get away with: about seventy decibels. What's wrong?

CARRIE. Nothing.

MATTHEW. Carrie, she can't hear us.

CARRIE. Yeah, because five minutes through the door I manage to repel her up the stairs.

MATTHEW. What are you talking about? She went to check on Emma.

CARRIE. It was just a joke. It's a natural reflex: if you're going to give me a set-up, then I'm going to deliver a punchline. Anyone who tells me that Father Christmas arrived with a full sack last night is going to get the same answer: 'That's because he only comes once a year!'

MATTHEW. Oh that. That was funny.

CARRIE. Then why didn't she laugh?

MATTHEW. She did.

CARRIE. That was a fake laugh.

MATTHEW. Honey, I've known Sheena since I was eleven, she wasn't pretending.

CARRIE. Really?

MATTHEW. Honestly.

CARRIE. Okay. I mean she married your brother so she must have a sense of humour.

MATTHEW. Carrie?

CARRIE. No, no I mean because he's funny. Not because he's funny peculiar, he's funny *funny*. And, you know, opposites attract so – not that she's *not* funny, I didn't mean she's not funny, she's, like, super-intelligent, and, and intense... ly clever, so maybe it was just too childish for her, maybe I should aim a little higher?

MATTHEW. Honey, don't over-analyse it. Maybe she's tired? Her daughter's really sick; she's got a lot on her mind. Don't take it personally. Just be yourself.

CARRIE. Yeah but sometimes 'myself' is a bit much, you know, for some people. Should I rein it in a bit? You can tell me, I won't mind. I know how much your family means to you. I should tone it down a bit, shouldn't I? You can say.

MATTHEW. Well, it's not rocket science, Carrie, just don't be vulgar.

CARRIE. Vulgar? You think I'm vulgar?

MATTHEW. No, I don't think you're vulgar.

CARRIE. Then who does? Did your mum call me vulgar?

MATTHEW. No, no, I just meant that the things we joke about together aren't necessarily the things to joke about in front of my family. Not everybody has the same sense of humour.

CARRIE. Yes, hello, I know that. I paid a lot of money to learn all about that. Do I walk into your office and tell you how to be a lawyer?

MATTHEW. No, but you'd ask me to tone it down if I went to stay with your family and dispensed legal advice five minutes after walking through the door.

Beat.

CARRIE. Wow. Say what you really feel, why don't you?

MATTHEW. Carrie –

CARRIE. You sure know how to make a girl feel better about herself.

MATTHEW. Honey, you just said I should be honest.

CARRIE. No, no, don't let me stop you. But on the subject of honesty, might I remind you, that if you wanted a wallflower for a girlfriend, you shouldn't have picked me!

Scene Two

The following rule is displayed to the audience for the duration of the scene:

Rule 1: Matthew must sit to tell a lie

When it is indicated that MATTHEW *either sits or stands, he must remain either seated or standing until stated otherwise.*

MATTHEW. Carrie, that's… that's what you got from what I just said? That I want a wallflower for a girlfriend? I didn't say that. I'd never say that. Honey, I'm sorry, I didn't mean to upset you. Hey, look at me. Carrie, honey, please don't do this, not today, it's Christmas –

CARRIE. I'm sorry. I hate being like this. I don't want to be this irritating, whining person. I just… I just really want your family to like me.

MATTHEW. I know, I know. (*Sitting.*) And they do. They do like you.

CARRIE. They don't know what to make of me. I'm never going to fit in.

MATTHEW (*remaining seated*). Of course you're going to fit in. You do. Fit in. Currently.

CARRIE. You're just saying that.

MATTHEW. I'm not just saying that.

CARRIE. What about your mum, what does she say about me? Does she say I'm funny?

MATTHEW (*standing*). Mum said you're always seeing the funny side of things.

CARRIE. And she said she liked that?

MATTHEW (*sitting*). Absolutely.

CARRIE. Really? Because I get the feeling she sees me as your… act of rebellion: in everything else you made the sensible decision. And then you met The Actress.

MATTHEW (*standing*). Carrie, we've been over this: before I went to law school I appeared in no less than fourteen amateur musicals. The only surprise to my family is that you're an actress not an actor. So just relax. This isn't an audition: you don't need to entertain them; you could just try talking to them. Or better yet, listen. As a general rule, people think you're a really interesting person if you let them talk *at you* about something of real interest *to them*.

They smile at each other.

CARRIE. I'm sorry that we keep having this same conversation.

MATTHEW (*sitting*). That's okay. I don't mind. We'll keep doing it until we get it right.

CARRIE. That's what you said to me the first time we made love.

MATTHEW (*standing*). Yeah, that's the kind of joke you can't make in front of my mother.

CARRIE. Got it. No probs. Hey, Matthew? I know I must drive you a bit nuts, but you're so patient with me, and I want you to know that after a whole year, I'm still so in love with you.

MATTHEW (*sitting beside her*). I'm still so in love with you too.

They kiss. SHEENA *enters.*

(*Standing, breaking away from* CARRIE.) Sheena! Hey, hey. How's Emma? Shall I go up?

SHEENA. Could you give her half an hour? She's just having a little rest.

MATTHEW. Sure, sure no problem. Whatever you want, whatever you need.

SHEENA (*referring to their contributions*). Well, look at all this: you've brought so much. These look… what are these?

CARRIE. Mince pies. I make them with filo pastry. It's more like a mince *parcel*.

SHEENA. A *mince parcel*, that's hilarious. I bet they're delicious.

MATTHEW (*sitting*). They really are.

CARRIE. Thanks, baby.

MATTHEW (*standing*). So how can we help? What can we do? Give us jobs.

SHEENA. Yes, jobs – wouldn't be Christmas without them. There's still a list as long as my arm despite your mother having it all prepared and in the freezer by last January!

SHEENA *and* MATTHEW *laugh. It unsettles* CARRIE; *she adjusts her appearance.*

Edith is the most organised woman you'll ever meet.

CARRIE. I've met her four times.

SHEENA. I know, I mean in general. Christmas Day in this house is carried out with military precision.

MATTHEW. There's a very strict timetable.

SHEENA. And she only uses the twenty-four-hour clock.

MATTHEW. We don't eat at 1 p.m., we eat at –

SHEENA/MATTHEW. Thirteen hundred hours!

SHEENA *and* MATTHEW *laugh.* CARRIE *smiles along; she adjusts her appearance.*

SHEENA. Actually we should get moving. Your mum's concerned there aren't enough carrots.

MATTHEW. That is concerning.

SHEENA. I know. And we haven't laid the table.

MATTHEW. Shay, I think that's a Code-Red Situation.

SHEENA. Crimson alert!

MATTHEW. Lock down the building. Evacuate non-essential personnel!

SHEENA *and* MATTHEW *share a generous laugh.*

CARRIE *laughs along and adjusts her appearance.*

SHEENA. So, Carrie, d'you want to do the carrots, and, Matt, you and I can lay the table? Carrots are in the bottom of the fridge; there should be a peeler in the utensil drawer.

MATTHEW. I'll get them for you.

SHEENA. D'you mind if I move your stuff off the table?

CARRIE. Oh, sure, sorry, I…

SHEENA. Carrie, why don't we move you… over here, is that all right?

CARRIE. Sure, of course.

MATTHEW (*fetching and delivering items to* CARRIE). Shay, has Mum said any more about Dad?

SHEENA. No, as far as I've heard he's recovering well. Adam can tell you more when he gets here.

MATTHEW. Where is he?

SHEENA. Oh, sorry, I should've said, we forgot the cranberry sauce. So Adam ran out to buy some, but that was an hour ago, so I can only assume he's actually foraging the hedgerows for cranberries. I'm sure he'll find his way home at some point between now and –

MATTHEW. The New Year!

MATTHEW *and* SHEENA *share another laugh.*

CARRIE *laughs too; she adjusts her appearance.*

SHEENA (*to* MATTHEW). It's so good to see you. (*Remembering* CARRIE.) Both of you. It's really good to see you. Both.

MATTHEW (*standing*). You too. You look well.

SHEENA. Do I? I don't feel it.

MATTHEW. You do. You look really well.

SHEENA. Oh thanks. Thank you. You always say the nicest things. (*Beat.*) Carrie?

CARRIE. Yes?

SHEENA. This is your first Christmas together as a couple, isn't it?

CARRIE. Yeah, it's a big step. We've been looking forward to it for ages, haven't we?

MATTHEW (*to* SHEENA). These side plates?

SHEENA. That's a cheese plate.

CARRIE. But enough about me, what about you, you're not with your family this year, obviously, because you're here.

SHEENA. I am.

CARRIE. You are.

SHEENA. My family's complicated: my parents are divorced.

CARRIE. Oh sorry…

SHEENA. It's not a sensitive issue. That said, Christmas negotiations are generally fraught – December's like a custody battle in my family.

MATTHEW *gives* SHEENA *an encouraging laugh.*

Matt knows. My parents are a nightmare, aren't they?

MATTHEW (*remaining standing*). They're… certainly opinionated.

SHEENA. Ever the diplomat. My parents are also lawyers; they can negotiate with everyone but each other. At my wedding – you remember?

MATTHEW. Of course I remember.

SHEENA. My mother actually interrupted the father-of-the-bride-speech by shouting –

MATTHEW/SHEENA. Objection!

MATTHEW *and* SHEENA *share another laugh.*

It unsettles CARRIE; *she adjusts her appearance.*

Scene Three

The following rules are displayed to the audience for the duration of the scene:

Rule 1. Matthew must sit to tell a lie

Rule 2. Carrie must stand to tell a joke

When it is stated that CARRIE *either sits or stands she must remain sitting or standing until stated otherwise.*

SHEENA *and* MATTHEW *stand to lay the table.* CARRIE *sits to peel carrots.*

SHEENA. He does such a good impression of my mum – you'd have to know her to appreciate it, but it's spot on. You're wasted as a solicitor, you should be on a stage.

MATTHEW (*sitting*). No I shouldn't.

SHEENA. I'll never forget your Major General in the *Pirates of Penzance* – you were fantastic!

MATTHEW (*standing*). Thanks, thank you. You say the nicest things.

SHEENA. That reminds me, Carrie, I can't tell you how much we enjoyed watching your TV show, the… the period drama…

CARRIE. *A Whisper of Autumn.*

SHEENA. *A Whisper of Autumn* – it was brilliant, you were brilliant.

CARRIE. It was only a small part.

SHEENA. It was a great part. Your character was really important – pivotal, actually – you poisoned the Archduke.

CARRIE. That was the scullery maid.

SHEENA. Of course it was, of course. You, you…

CARRIE. Stole the letter.

SHEENA. You stole the letter. Exactly. And if you hadn't done that then, then… it wouldn't… none of it would have been the same. Would it?

CARRIE. Well… I suppose he wouldn't have met the Countess. She was great, wasn't she?

SHEENA. She's a great actress, she's properly brilliant. Isn't she?

MATTHEW. Oh yeah, she's properly brilliant.

SHEENA. So funny.

MATTHEW. And witty.

CARRIE. Well that's the script. I had some pretty funny lines, too –

SHEENA. It's her timing, maybe, or her expression.

CARRIE. – I was quite lucky.

MATTHEW. She has a great face.

SHEENA. Such a great face.

CARRIE (*standing*). 'It wasn't just his purse that was small, if you take my meaning!'

Beat.

SHEENA. Oh yes, yes that was your line. I remember, it was great. Well done.

CARRIE (*sitting*). Thanks, thank you.

SHEENA. So what's next, is there anything else on the horizon?

CARRIE. Well, not just at the moment… it's totally normal to have periods where you're not working.

SHEENA. Sure, of course. (*Beat.*) And, Matt, how's work, I've been dying to know, have they offered you – [partnership]?

CARRIE. Actually I had an audition in New York. It was a complete disaster… (*Standing.*) But it's a really funny story, isn't it?

MATTHEW (*sitting*). Hilarious.

CARRIE (*remaining standing*). I was so jetlagged when I got off the plane that I walked into my audition in a complete daze. I sat down, unbuttoned my coat, started my spiel: 'Hi, so great to meet you, blah blah blah', when suddenly they started looking at me with these horrified expressions and I realised, hang on a second, didn't I take my coat off in the hall? Underneath my coat I'd been wearing a tea dress with buttons up the front. I looked down and I was sat there in my tights and my bra. I had hung my dress over the back of the chair. Yeah, yeah, I was sat there half-naked in front of the entire production team!

SHEENA (*laughing genuinely*). Oh Carrie, I'm sorry to laugh.

CARRIE (*sitting*). You're supposed to laugh, it's funny – humiliating, but funny.

SHEENA. I would've had an absolute sense of humour failure.

CARRIE (*standing*). Well it could have been worse; at least I was wearing a bra!

SHEENA *laughs harder.* CARRIE *sits, relieved.*

SHEENA. Carrie, you're hilarious. She's hilarious. How do the two of you ever get anything done?

MATTHEW (*standing*). With difficulty most of the time.

ADAM *enters, holding aloft a jar of redcurrant jelly and a plastic bag.*

ADAM. All hail the conquering hero!

MATTHEW (*remaining stood*). The hunter-gatherer returns!

ADAM. There he is, there's my favourite brother.

MATTHEW. There's my *only* brother.

ADAM. Come here and give us a kiss, then.

The brothers embrace heartily.

Hang on a minute, who's this? What've you done with my little brother? There's hardly anything left of him. Look at you – you've been working out.

MATTHEW. I've been trying to eat healthily.

SHEENA. Matt, yes, you look great!

ADAM (*to* CARRIE). You watch this one; don't let him disappear. Come here, gorgeous.

CARRIE. Happy Christmas.

ADAM. You're looking festive.

CARRIE. Am I?

ADAM. You look like the front-window display of Hamleys!

CARRIE (*standing*). Just the look I was going for.

ADAM. Nailed it.

CARRIE (*remaining stood, high-fiving*). Nailed it!

> ADAM *and* CARRIE *share a laugh;* SHEENA *adjusts her appearance.* CARRIE *sits.*

SHEENA. Adam, did you get the milk for Emma?

ADAM (*fetching the milk*). The supermarket was closed, so I found this on the back shelves in a village shop. It's covered in dust, but we can wipe it down.

CARRIE (*standing*). That's what Matthew said to me the first time we made love! (*Sitting.*) Sorry, too much?

ADAM. Carrie, something you need to learn about this family: we don't take ourselves too seriously.

SHEENA. Hey, Adam?

ADAM. Yup?

SHEENA. I asked for rice milk this is goat's milk.

ADAM. Shay, it's Christmas Day, nobody's selling rice milk. It's a miracle I found that.

MATTHEW. Why's Emma drinking goat's milk?

SHEENA. We're restricting her diet to see if she has allergies. No sugar, no gluten, no lactose.

CARRIE (*standing*). No fun!

SHEENA. I know, but it's not about fun, it's about health.

CARRIE (*sitting*). Sure, sorry, I…

ADAM. Shay, goat's milk is fine.

SHEENA. Goat's milk has lactose in it.

ADAM. Far less than in cow's milk.

SHEENA. Adam, I've done the research. These things affect the microbiome. Your internal gut fauna.

ADAM. Flora.

SHEENA. Flora. Which governs your immune system. And it undoubtedly makes a difference.

ADAM. I looked it up, too: many lactose-intolerant people drink goat's milk. It'll be fine. It's just for *one day*.

Scene Four

The following rules are displayed to the audience for the duration of the scene:

Rule 1. Matthew must sit to tell a lie

Rule 2. Carrie must stand to tell a joke

Rule 3. Sheena must drink to contradict

When it's stated that SHEENA *drinks, one sip or gulp will suffice unless stated otherwise.*

SHEENA. Sure, fine, if you say so. It's important not to get too pedantic about these things.

ADAM. Thank you. (*Beat.*) So, where's Mum? Still paying homage to the Sky Fairy?

SHEENA. She'll be back in about ten – so we should get a move on.

ADAM. Just enough time for a cheeky lager. I may have hidden a secret stash in the cold box.

CARRIE. Why's it a secret?

MATTHEW. Dad has a thing about lager.

ADAM. He's a 'real ale' man, our dad.

CARRIE (*standing*). Oooh, bootleg beer! (*Taking the beer, sitting.*) Thank you.

MATTHEW (*taking a beer*). All right, thanks. (*Offering it to* SHEENA.) Shay, d'you want this one?

ADAM *and* SHEENA *share a look.*

SHEENA. No, thank you, I'm going to try and pace myself. I want to avoid that situation where you realise you've had five drinks and the turkey hasn't even come out the oven.

MATTHEW (*sitting*). You never do that.

SHEENA. I've been accused of doing that in the past.

MATTHEW (*sitting*). That's nonsense. (*Standing.*) Are you sure you won't have one?

SHEENA. Yes, I'm absolutely sure. Actually, I haven't had a drink all week, and you know something, I feel great – I mean my skin is clearer, I'm sleeping much better, yeah, I know, so… I mean I *may* have a glass of wine with lunch, but otherwise I'm just not interested.

CARRIE. Good for you.

MATTHEW (*handing back his beer*). I'll go without, too. Beer is pretty calorific.

ADAM. I need those calories to keep me off the fags.

MATTHEW. You've quit?

ADAM. Cut back, yeah. One a day. Two a day. It's going well – easier than I thought.

MATTHEW. Wow, you guys, that's… you're really making changes.

Beat; SHEENA *and* ADAM *look at one another.*

CARRIE. I'll drink to that. (*Standing*.) I'm in the middle of a *change* reaction! No? No one with me? I mean I could go for something more traditional if you want? Yup? Okay. Cheers!

ADAM. Cheers!

CARRIE *sits*.

MATTHEW. Adam, what's the update on Dad – any news?

ADAM. Not much. Mum said he was recovering well, but that he's had a bit of a setback. I don't really know what that means. Apparently it's fairly normal. He'll be fine – Dad has the constitution of an ox.

MATTHEW. Yeah, he can come back from anything.

ADAM. Mum said three days after the operation he was lecturing the nurses on the 'inherent superiority of imperial measurements'.

MATTHEW. Typical Dad – he'll be giving orders to his funeral director from inside the coffin.

ADAM. He'll be giving orders to *our* funeral directors from inside the grave.

The brothers laugh.

It's great that he's coming home.

MATTHEW. Yeah, it's going to be so good to see him.

ADAM. It'll be great to all be together, one big family, won't it? (*Putting an arm around* SHEENA.) We mustn't take it for granted. Dad's right when he says family is not just an important thing, it's everything. Don't you agree, honey?

ADAM *takes a swig of his beer;* SHEENA *looks at it enviously.*

SHEENA (*burying the urge to contradict*). Yes of course, family is the most important thing there is.

MATTHEW. So how long are you guys staying?

SHEENA (*extricating herself from* ADAM*'s arm*). I was planning to head home this evening.

MATTHEW. Oh no, why? Why so soon?

SHEENA. Adam and I agreed that Emma should sleep in her own bed tonight.

MATTHEW. But Emma loves staying here.

ADAM. He's right, she does. Hey, we could try and get her up to Shepherd's Lookout tomorrow.

SHEENA *fiddles with the beer can*.

MATTHEW. Emma loves the view from that hill.

ADAM. Let's stay the night, head back tomorrow, it hardly makes a difference, does it?

SHEENA (*raising the can, readying to drink*). Adam, I really don't want to cause a disagreement –

ADAM. Then don't. Course we'll stay. It'll mean so much to Dad. You don't have a problem with that, do you, Shay?

SHEENA (*putting down the beer can*). No, no problem at all, no objections from me.

EDITH (*calling from off*). Hello…?

ADAM *and* CARRIE *quickly ditch their beer cans. ADAM hands his to* MATTHEW, *who is forced to hide it behind his back as* EDITH *enters from the corridor.*

Hello! Oh you're here! You're here!

MATTHEW. Hi, Mum!

EDITH. Hi, darling. Happy Christmas!

MATTHEW. Happy Christmas, Mum.

EDITH. Oh look at you: there's nothing left of you! You look fantastic. Your father will be pleased.

CARRIE. Hello, Edith.

EDITH. Carrie, darling, Happy Christmas!

CARRIE. Happy Christmas! (*Standing.*) Can I please give you one of my famously tiny hugs!

CARRIE envelops EDITH in an enormous embrace; it aggravates EDITH's bad back.

EDITH. Oh how lovely… how lovely…

EDITH extricates herself from the hug. CARRIE sits.

Carrie, I was just delighted when Matthew told me you'd asked to come. Really delighted. Thrilled. Isn't it wonderful to have Carrie?

ADAM. Yeah, it's great.

SHEENA. It's really great.

EDITH. It's really great.

Beat.

MATTHEW. How was church, Mum?

EDITH. Oh it was a huge crowd – such a turnout of young. Tom and Sarah were there with their two girls. (*To* CARRIE.) Tom's a school friend of Adam's. His eldest must be Emma's age – maybe a bit older, fifteen maybe? I didn't expect to see them, Tom has a new job in Geneva – frighteningly clever man – but they all turned out in their Christmas best to be with their old mum, the whole family in the pew together, isn't that nice? And all the children were given an orange with a candle stuck into it and they all processed down the aisle – it was too sweet.

CARRIE. Why an orange?

EDITH. Do you know, I'm not entirely sure, but I imagine it must represent something.

CARRIE (*standing*). It's probably because they're –

MATTHEW (*pushing CARRIE back down into her seat*). Mum, Carrie made mince pies.

EDITH. Oh wonderful, darling, Sheena made a batch, but we were worried there weren't enough – only half of them survived the journey.

CARRIE. Oh, you made some, too?

SHEENA. Yes, gluten-free.

EDITH. Right, where's my list? (*Reading from the list and crossing off as she goes*.) Let's see where we are, what time is it? Right, the turkey will come out to rest at twenty to one, and we'll eat at one o'clock. That's right, after last year – (*Directed at* ADAM.) when I received such a ribbing for my timetable –

ADAM. I didn't say anything.

EDITH. – I've now switched to the twelve-hour clock, and I've built leeway into the schedule, okay? Even your old mum can adapt and change, all right? (*Returning to the list*.) Now, who's done me some more carrots?

CARRIE. I have. I've cut them lengthways, is that –

EDITH. Darling, would you mind not using that peeler? It's really a citrus-rind peeler and a carrot will blunt it.

CARRIE. Oh sorry, I didn't realise…

MATTHEW. It's my fault, I gave it to her.

EDITH *moves to the dishwasher to retrieve the correct peeler*.

EDITH. I'll get you another one, it's just that little bit more robust. Who loaded the dishwasher?

ADAM. Uh-oh.

EDITH. Who loaded the dishwasher?

MATTHEW. Mum, don't get cross.

EDITH. I'm not cross. I just want to know who put these knives in the dishwasher?

CARRIE. I… I did.

EDITH (*approaching*). This is silver, this is stainless steel. You see the difference? Under no circumstances does the silver go in the dishwasher.

CARRIE. I'm really sorry.

EDITH. That's fine, dear, you won't do it again. (*Giving* CARRIE *the correct peeler*.) That's right, slice them lengthways, maybe a wee bit less stumpy… and we'll toss them with the parsnips, and pop them in to roast twenty minutes after the potatoes, which have been prepared in advance. That's the secret to any successful lunch party: everything that can be done the day before *must* be done the day before. That's the only rule. That and a decent knife-sharpener – best investment you'll ever make. Is your mother the same, does she get everything ready in advance?

CARRIE. Actually we have Christmas dinner, so we have the whole day to cook.

EDITH. Christmas dinner is a lovely thing to do, but it's impractical with children. Instead we fill the day with fun: Francis always loves to play a game before lunch. Each year he nominates someone to bring a new game. Last year Adam brought Twister which was… physically challenging. But this year it's Matthew's turn.

MATTHEW. I brought a card game. I think Dad'll love it. You have to follow all these absurd rules, and it starts out simple but descends into madness!

EDITH. Oh that sounds… interesting. We'll see what your father says.

CARRIE. I'm so looking forward to meeting Francis – Matt's told me so much about him.

EDITH. And he's so looking forward to meeting you. (*Noticing* CARRIE*'s mobile phone.*) Oh, we have a sort of little 'house rule' for whenever we sit down to a meal together: no electronics. Francis is very strict on this point.

CARRIE. Oh I completely agree – nothing worse than having your meal interrupted by an obnoxious ringtone… (*Standing and imitating an obnoxious ring tone. Sitting.*) It's awful isn't it?

EDITH. Exactly… (*Returning to her list, crossing off as she goes.*) Sprouts are done. Potatoes – oh yes, Francis has never liked roast potatoes, so I make him a side of mash. Can somebody bear to do the mashing for me, I know it's a boring job.

MATTHEW. I'll do it.

EDITH. Oh Matthew, my martyr, thank you. (*Returning to the list*.) Right, drinks: help yourselves to beer – I've stocked the fridge.

ADAM. Is it real ale, Mum?

EDITH. Of course.

ADAM. Oh that sounds good, doesn't it? Who'd like a lovely *real ale*?

EDITH. Yes, you must.

CARRIE. Yes please, I fancy some real ale.

ADAM. Me too, I haven't had a drink all day.

ADAM *pours a real ale for himself and* CARRIE; SHEENA *watches, irked*.

EDITH. Sheena, can you please decant and taste the red wine for me?

MATTHEW. I can do that.

EDITH. No, it needs Sheena – it's a vintage and it'd be awful if it had turned. I'll finish the table because I know how it's supposed to be, and you can taste the wine because… Red wine's your poison, isn't it?

SHEENA. Apparently so.

SHEENA *begins to open a bottle of wine*.

EDITH (*returning to her list*). Now, yes, logs. (*To* ADAM.) You know Dad loves a fire, can I put you in charge? Decorations. Yes: the tree. I couldn't do the top because of my back, so would you boys please find time to finish it off? What would your father say if he saw it in that state? Adam, make a start. (*Returning to the list*.) Now, what have I forgotten? Oh yes: Dad! He's being dropped off by the nurses at twelve thirty.

MATTHEW. How is he, Mum?

EDITH. Oh heavens!

SHEENA. What?

EDITH. The pudding – I forgot the Christmas pudding!

CARRIE. Don't worry, Christmas pudding's horrible anyway.

EDITH. No, I made one. I just forgot to put it on to boil. We'll have to microwave it. Right, troops, we've got under an hour and a lot to get through so man your stations!

They all get on with their assigned tasks.

Oh Adam, tell Matthew your good news.

ADAM. What news?

EDITH. Your article. Adam has just had an article published!

MATTHEW. Hey, that's fantastic.

CARRIE. In what, a newspaper?

ADAM. No, just a… a law review.

MATTHEW. That's really great, congratulations.

ADAM. Thanks.

CARRIE. Matthew's got some good news, too.

EDITH. Oh yes?

MATTHEW. We can talk about it later. Carrie, later –

CARRIE. Matthew has been offered partnership by his firm!

EDITH. What?

SHEENA. Oh my God…!

EDITH. No! Is that true? Matthew, that's wonderful! Oh your father will be thrilled!

Scene Five

The following rules are displayed to the audience for the duration of the scene:

Rule 1. Matthew must sit to tell a lie

Rule 2. Carrie must stand to tell a joke

Rule 3. Sheena must drink to contradict

Rule 4. Adam must affect an accent to mock

Where it is stated that ADAM *must affect an accent the actor must feel free to adopt a variety of accents, intonations and silly voices or stick to just one, whichever is preferred. The actor must also feel free to accent the whole sentence or just highlight certain words, whichever is preferred.*

EDITH. Gosh, that's young to be a partner, isn't it? How old are you?

MATTHEW (*remaining stood*). You don't know how old I am?

CARRIE (*remaining seated*). Thirty-six.

EDITH. Still, that's very young. Adam is forty-two, and he's not yet –

MATTHEW. Adam started later than I did – too busy playing for England in his twenties.

SHEENA. Congratulations, that's amazing. Adam, don't you want to congratulate your brother?

ADAM. Hey, yeah, that's… it's amazing. You should be proud. Congratulations.

MATTHEW (*standing*). Thanks, thank you. And that's great news about your article. What's it about?

ADAM. It's not important.

EDITH. Of course it's important – tell him what it's about.

MATTHEW. Tell me.

ADAM. Healthcare Litigation Financing and the Management of Risk.

Beat.

MATTHEW/CARRIE/EDITH. Great, that's great. / That sounds really clever. / Isn't that great?

EDITH. It had some really good jokes. What was that one about the, the… it was a sports metaphor.

ADAM. It doesn't matter

MATTHEW/EDITH. No, tell us. / Tell him.

ADAM (*affecting an accent*). 'Every time the surgeons hit the lawyers for six, the judicial system moves the boundary!' Wahey!

EDITH. Isn't it good?

MATTHEW. Very good, very nice.

CARRIE. I'm not sure I get it.

MATTHEW. He's referring to the fact that surgeons are always getting sued. But every time they win the law changes so they can continue to be sued.

CARRIE. Oh… yes, okay, that's funny.

ADAM (*affecting an accent*). Cutting-edge comedy: legal wordplay!

EDITH. It's a really good piece of writing – you're a good writer.

ADAM. It's no big deal – I didn't spend much time on it.

SHEENA. He's right, he didn't.

EDITH. Well, I'm just so proud of both my boys. And so is your father. We're very lucky to have two equally brilliant sons. Matthew, you've found a way to put your acting talents to such good use.

ADAM (*affecting an accent*). 'There's more money to be made when you're called to the bar than when you're treading the boards.'

MATTHEW. Dad was always saying that.

EDITH. Dad was right. He said you'd excel as a lawyer and look at how well that's worked out for you. (*To* ADAM.) And you as well, darling, it's all worked out for the best, hasn't it?

ADAM (*affecting an accent*). I'd have hated to be a famous cricketer – it would've been a real drag!

EDITH. Fame is a curse. I look at some of these television sports people and I feel sorry for them: there's no privacy. Think of how it would've affected Emma. You'd be off to Australia, Sri Lanka –

ADAM (*affecting an accent*). Sounds hideous!

MATTHEW (*sitting*). Ghastly!

EDITH. You wouldn't be having Christmas here with your family, would you? And family is not just an important thing –

ADAM/MATTHEW (MATTHEW *stands,* ADAM *affects an accent*). It's everything!

EDITH. Your father taught you that.

MATTHEW. How is he, Mum?

EDITH. He's fine, darling. (*To* ADAM.) Adam, is that what you're wearing?

ADAM (*affecting an accent*). Apparently not.

EDITH. What would your father say? Come on, wear a shirt.

MATTHEW. Mum, tell us about Dad, how is he?

EDITH. He's healing really well – the doctor assures me that he stands every chance of making a full recovery. He just needs to stay positive and that's what we're for.

MATTHEW. Sure, sure.

ADAM. Of course.

EDITH. After everything he's done for us the least we can do is try really hard to make this the perfect Christmas Day for him!

SHEENA/MATTHEW/ADAM/CARRIE. Of course. / We won't let him down. / He can count on us. / Absolutely.

EDITH. Right, quickly, no more chatting, we've got so much to get through! Sheena, can you get on and taste the wine? It's Dad's favourite and I couldn't bear it if it had spoiled.

SHEENA *tastes the wine, she swills it round her mouth.*

Tell me it's fine – it's fine, isn't it?

SHEENA *spits it out into a glass.*

SHEENA. Yes, it's fine. It's delicious.

EDITH. Oh good. Dad'll be delighted. (*Referring to the table.*) Hold on a minute. Sheena, you've forgotten a place. We're seven. There are seven of us. Matthew, Adam, Francis, the three of us and Emma. That makes seven.

SHEENA (*drinking and swallowing*). No, actually, we're six. Emma won't be joining us for lunch; she needs to stay in bed.

Scene Six

The following rules are disclosed to the audience for the duration of the scene:

Rule 1. Matthew must sit to tell a lie

Rule 2. Carrie must stand to tell a joke

Rule 3. Sheena must drink to contradict

Rule 4. Adam must affect an accent to mock

Rule 5. Edith must clean to keep calm

The general idea is that EDITH*'s cleaning becomes increasingly thorough and obsessive over time.* EDITH *may hum or sing to herself, from time to time, as she cleans – whatever necessary to calm herself.*

EDITH. Emma won't be joining us for lunch?

SHEENA. I'm sorry, Edith, but she's just not well enough. We're under strict instructions from her doctor. He says that busy social situations overwhelm her.

EDITH. I'd hardly call a quiet lunch with the family a 'busy social situation'.

SHEENA. Well… (*Drinking*.) Actually it is. We're trying to establish her 'Energy Envelope'. We need to know how much is in the envelope before we ask her to stretch herself. I'm sorry.

EDITH. Don't apologise to me, it doesn't matter a bit to me, it's Francis I worry about, who knows how often he'll get to have Christmas lunch with his granddaughter in the future? But I suppose that's not important, we can just explain: 'Sorry, you can't spend time with your granddaughter on the most important day of the year, because she's a bit sleepy and she'd rather take a nap!'

EDITH *begins to clean; she cleans throughout the following*.

MATTHEW. Mum…?

SHEENA (*drinking*). Actually, it's rather more serious than that. We think we finally have a diagnosis.

MATTHEW. What? When was this?

SHEENA. They think she has Chronic Fatigue Syndrome.

CARRIE. What does that mean?

ADAM (*affecting an accent*). It means she's fatigued chronically.

SHEENA. It means that she's persistently tired to the point of not being able to function normally.

MATTHEW. Was this recently? Why didn't you tell me? I mean *us*, why didn't you tell *us*?

CARRIE. What causes it?

ADAM. They don't really know. Sometimes it starts after a virus, but she never had a virus.

MATTHEW. How do they treat it?

SHEENA. Rest, mainly. And… therapy.

CARRIE. Therapy?

SHEENA. It's a medical condition with associated psychiatric symptoms.

EDITH. Whose shoes are these?

MATTHEW. What do you mean 'psychiatric symptoms'?

SHEENA. We've been talking to a therapist, a cognitive behavioural therapist. CBT is a good therapy style for treating anxiety.

EDITH. Whose shoes are these, please?

SHEENA. We think she might be suffering from adrenal stress because of excessive anxiety.

CARRIE. Why?

SHEENA. Well that's what we're trying to understand.

CARRIE. What d'you think is making her anxious?

ADAM (*affecting an accent*). That is what we're trying to understand, Carrie.

SHEENA. She has very low self-esteem.

EDITH (*without cleaning, without calm*). Unless somebody claims these, I'm going to throw them out.

ADAM. They're mine.

EDITH. Put them on or put them away, please.

EDITH *resumes cleaning*.

MATTHEW. Carry on, Shay.

SHEENA (*drinking*). No, I don't think now's the time.

MATTHEW. Yes it is. Mum, come and sit down, we need to talk about this as a family. It's important. Mum?

EDITH. All right, all right, I'm coming.

EDITH *stops cleaning and sits at the table with* SHEENA.

MATTHEW. Explain from the beginning, Shay. We're all here for you, we're all listening. What is this Cognitive…?

SHEENA. Cognitive Behavioural Therapy.

MATTHEW. Right.

SHEENA. Well… it's a type of therapy they often recommend for people suffering from anxiety or depression. The idea is…

MATTHEW. Go on.

SHEENA. I'm no expert, but the gist of it is – anxious or depressed people tend to have very negative 'core beliefs' about themselves. 'I'm useless', 'I'm worthless', 'I'm unlovable', that sort of thing.

MATTHEW. Sure, sure, yeah…

EDITH *begins to clean the cutlery/glasses on the table.*

SHEENA. And CBT helps you to… change those 'core beliefs'. Or at least to manage them.

MATTHEW. So Emma has negative core beliefs?

SHEENA. She believes she's inadequate.

CARRIE. No…

MATTHEW. In what way?

SHEENA. In… just about every way.

MATTHEW. But she's wonderful.

SHEENA. I know, of course she is. But that's not how she sees herself – and it colours every interaction she has, with anyone, every day. If she, say… waves at a friend across the street and they don't wave back, or someone snaps at her in school, or, her father teases her –

ADAM. Hey, she knows I'm only joking.

SHEENA. – she automatically assumes that it's because she's somehow not good enough. In fact, she takes it as *further* evidence that she's inadequate. So it's like a feedback loop. And she's undermining herself so much that it's making her ill.

EDITH. She should spend more time outdoors.

ADAM. Well I'm trying – we're hoping that she'll agree to walk up to Shepherd's Lookout tomorrow.

EDITH. She works too hard, that's her problem.

SHEENA. She does, because she's trying to compensate for feeling inadequate. According to the therapist, even when you have a low opinion of yourself you still have to get on with life and so you create 'rules for living' to help you through the day.

MATTHEW. Like what?

SHEENA. Like demanding of yourself that you must be the best, or the most beautiful or most successful – that kind of thing.

EDITH *gets up from the table to clean the room.*

MATTHEW. So what's Emma's?

SHEENA. She thinks she must be perfect.

MATTTHEW. But nobody's perfect.

CARRIE (*standing*). I am. (*Sitting.*) I'm not. Sorry, carry on.

SHEENA. She thinks if she gets the perfect grades; if she has the perfect friends; if she says and does everything perfectly then maybe no one will notice that she's not good enough.

EDITH (*cleaning*). Some rules are helpful: eat your greens; be on time; respect your elders – if we had no rules there'd be anarchy.

SHEENA. Yes… (*Drinking.*) But. A rule that might seem helpful to begin with can actually become toxic.

MATTHEW. Yeah, no, yeah…

SHEENA. For example, a girl might start out wanting to lose a little weight – so she sets a rule: 'If I lose weight, people will find me more attractive.' And at first it may even work – people say she's looking great. But then she keeps going – 'If I lose *more* weight, people will like me even more…' And before you know it, she's anorexic.

ADAM (*affecting an accent*). At ease, Matthew.

MATTHEW. Hey… some of us are trying to listen here. Shay?

SHEENA. Emma started out trying to get better marks at school. Get on the hockey team. Do well at violin. We thought she was thriving, everyone was praising her – as far as she was concerned, her rule was working. But she couldn't stop. She just kept going to more and more extreme lengths.

EDITH *begins to hum as she cleans*.

MATTHEW. Like what?

SHEENA. Staying up all night, trying to do the perfect art project, the perfect essay… having panic attacks about every test… trying to get onto *every* team, which isn't even possible.

ADAM. We did try to tell her to slow down, it's not like –

SHEENA. Of course we did – but she couldn't. If she let her grades slip even a little, she thought everyone would start blaming her. She thought the perfectionism was *solving* her problems, rather than *causing* them.

EDITH*'s cleaning becomes disruptive*. SHEENA *has to work hard to get her point across*.

What she really needed to do was confront her core belief – to realise that people like her for who she is, not for what she achieves. But what she actually did was try harder and harder to meet the terms of her rule in order to disguise her true self from everybody.

MATTHEW. No wonder she's exhausted.

SHEENA. Exactly, and now on the verge of a complete psychological breakdown!

EDITH *lets out a gasp of pain and clutches her back*.

MATTHEW. Mum? Mum, what are you doing? Stop that or you'll put your back out.

EDITH *continues to clean despite the pain in her back*.

Let me do that, go and talk to Sheena. Give me that and go and sit down.

MATTHEW *stops his mother from cleaning. Unable to clean, she's unable to keep calm.*

EDITH (*without cleaning, without calm*). Actually I'd love to sit and talk, Matthew, but we can't all sit around all day because somebody has to get ready for your father's arrival.

MATTHEW. I know, but it's important to talk about Emma's illness.

EDITH (*without cleaning, without calm*). Well in my day we never had such a thing. You couldn't just stay in bed all day. Our parents wouldn't hear of it. They'd have called you lazy!

MATTHEW. Mum –

EDITH (*without cleaning, without calm*). When I was fourteen I was raising my sisters. Three of them. With an absent father and mother ill in bed. Do you imagine I didn't want to curl up on the sofa and have someone talk to me about my 'Energy Envelope'? No, I just had to get on with it, didn't I? I didn't have a choice! (*Cleaning, calming.*) Darlings, whose bags are these? Are they yours?

MATTHEW. Yes, don't lift them, I'll do it.

EDITH (*cleaning*). Carrie, I'm sorry, but I haven't had time to make up the bed in the best spare for you. Would you mind giving me a hand? It puts my back out to do it alone.

CARRIE. The best spare… room?

EDITH (*cleaning*). Yes, House Rules I'm afraid. I know it's rather old-fashioned, but Francis is a traditional man. And until you're married… I hope you understand.

CARRIE. Oh right… sure, of course. (*Standing.*) But you needn't worry, there's no risk of Matthew and me 'living in sin' – he'd have to ask me to move in with him first!

EDITH, MATTHEW *and* CARRIE *exit.*

ADAM. Thanks for agreeing to stay the night, I know it wasn't the deal.

SHEENA. You're right, it wasn't the deal.

ADAM. I know, but Mum really appreciates it. I really
    appreciate it. And it gives us some time to… D'you know the
    first thing Emma said to me when I arrived this morning?

SHEENA. Adam, please –

ADAM. She said, 'I miss you, Daddy, when are you coming
    home?'

    MATTHEW *enters carrying the log basket.* ADAM *puts an
    arm around* SHEENA.

    (*Affecting an accent.*) Are you and Carrie looking forward to
    a little Victorian-era corridor-creeping tonight?

SHEENA (*untangling herself from* ADAM*'s embrace*). Adam's
    volunteered to sleep on the floor in Emma's room to keep her
    company, so you won't be the only ones sleeping alone.

    Beat.

MATTHEW. Mum said to remind you to get the logs.

ADAM. Trade you the logs for the potatoes.

MATTHEW. Already done. Anyhow, I don't think it's wise to
    deviate from The Plan.

ADAM (*taking the log basket*). Sure… (*To* SHEENA.) Let's
    stick to *the plan*, then, shall we?

    MATTHEW *looks between* ADAM *and* SHEENA, *confused.*
    ADAM *exits to the garden.*

MATTHEW. Alone at last… Shay, look, I'm so sorry about
    Emma. It makes me feel desperate to think of her so
    unhappy. But it's good you have a diagnosis.

SHEENA. Well, that didn't go down so well with your mum.

MATTHEW. Oh she was just… just give her a bit of time.
    She'll be… just give her time. Look, why don't I get you a
    glass of wine?

SHEENA. Matt…

MATTHEW. Come on, one small glass of wine isn't going to
    hurt anybody. And let's be honest, Christmas is a lot easier
    with a glass of wine inside you. You know I'm right.

SHEENA. Go on then, just one. But if I'm going to break my Christmas resolution, then you have to break yours: have a mince pie. They're gluten- and sugar-free – fewer calories.

MATTHEW. All right, but don't tell Carrie – she'd be mad at me if she knew I didn't have one of hers.

SHEENA. Don't tell Adam – I promised him I wouldn't.

MATTHEW. Scout's honour. It'll be our little secret.

MATTHEW *pours* SHEENA *a glass of wine;* SHEENA *fetches* MATTHEW *a mince pie.*

So, look, I know Emma's illness isn't the only thing upsetting you. Come on then, spill the beans – I've been wanting to ask since the moment I saw you: what happened with you and Adam?

SHEENA. What d'you mean?

MATTHEW. When we last spoke on the phone… I've never heard you so upset.

SHEENA *stares at the glass of wine being poured.*

SHEENA. Was I? Was I really?

MATTHEW *puts down the bottle of wine to labour his point.*

MATTHEW. Yes. And then you didn't call me back, so I had no idea what was going on.

SHEENA. D'you want me to pour that?

MATTHEW (*pouring the wine*). I didn't know if you were even going to come today. I thought maybe that was it, maybe you'd packed your bags and walked out.

SHEENA. What…? (*Reaching eagerly for the glass, drinking.*) No, no that was never going to happen. Look, I really shouldn't have told you in the first place – I was making a mountain out of a molehill. Everything's back to normal now; in fact, it's like it never happened.

Scene Seven

The following rules are disclosed to the audience for the duration of the scene:

Rule 1. Matthew must sit **and eat** to tell a lie

Rule 2. Carrie must stand to tell a joke

Rule 3. Sheena must drink to contradict

Rule 4. Adam must affect an accent to mock

Rule 5. Edith must clean to keep calm

When it is stated that MATTHEW *eats, a small mouthful will suffice.*

MATTHEW. Really? Cos just now I got the impression that there was still something the matter.

SHEENA. Did you…? (*Drinking*.) No, nothing's the matter. (*Referring to the wine*.) This really is delicious –

MATTHEW. I could sense a bit of tension.

SHEENA. – I've always like a good claret… (*Drinking*.) Uh-uh, nope, no tension at all, it was a bump in the road that's all. I'm sorry to worry you, were you really worried?

MATTHEW. Did you…? (*Sitting, eating*.) Yes… Yes I was. You had me really worried.

SHEENA. Well we're fine, so you don't need to worry any more, do you?

MATTHEW (*continuing to sit and eat*). No… No, that's great, that's… great news. I'm delighted for you. You guys are the best. I've always been rooting for you. I'd have been devastated if anything happened to you guys… (*Standing*.) I mean I was running all these… simulations and, and… (*Sitting, eating*.) None of them were good. Nope. No. So this is… excellent and, and… (*Standing*.) As it should be. This is exactly as it should be.

SHEENA. How's the mince pie? Any good?

MATTHEW (*sitting, eating*). It's delicious.

SHEENA. Really? Not too dry?

MATTHEW (*continuing to sit and eat*). No, no, not dry at all.

SHEENA. Oh good, good. You know, Matt, it really is great news about your promotion –

MATTHEW (*standing*). Shay, I don't mean to pry, but how exactly did you guys sort it out?

SHEENA. Look, I really shouldn't. I got in enough trouble for telling you in the first place.

MATTHEW. Adam told you off for telling me? What is this, Stasi Germany?

SHEENA. Shh – seventy decibels.

MATTHEW (*lowering his voice*). What's his problem? We didn't do anything wrong.

SHEENA. Of course we didn't, but he's your brother and it's not fair to either of you.

MATTHEW. Hey, come on, I've known you as long as he has. Who gave me my first cigarette? Who made me smoke menthol cigarettes in the back garden when I was eleven?

SHEENA. Right.

MATTHEW. Right, it was you, it's always been you... I mean, I know you, so stop being so distant, it's weird not talking. Tell me.

SHEENA. Okay, fine, but you have to pretend you don't know.

MATTHEW (*remaining standing*). I can do that. That won't be a problem for me.

SHEENA. It was our anniversary a couple of weeks ago and we'd decided to go to a hotel and give Emma to my mum. And he, he just didn't book anywhere, and it was the night before and he hadn't booked a hotel and so we just stayed at home. And it's not just our anniversary – this past couple of years he hasn't made an effort in anything. And what I don't understand, okay, is why, why didn't he book a hotel? Is it, A: because he doesn't give a shit about me; is it B: because he's moronically incapable of making a decision; or is it C: because he's having some kind of midlife crisis? Which? Which is it? I don't know. That's what I want to know. Because if it's A –

MATTHEW. And A is…?

SHEENA. A: he doesn't give a shit about me.

MATTHEW. Right.

SHEENA. Then that's fine, that's okay – we can part company and call it a day. But if he does give a shit. If it's B or C then why doesn't he bloody well say something? That's what I want to know. Why can't he just tell me?

The back door opens – immediately MATTHEW *and* SHEENA *swap over the mince pie and the glass of wine.* ADAM *enters.*

(*Sitting, eating.*) Oh so that's why you have to water your Christmas tree.

MATTHEW (*standing, drinking*). What…?

SHEENA (*sitting, eating*). I didn't know they were so highly combustible.

MATTHEW. Well, yes, wood…

SHEENA. Can spontaneously burst into flames.

MATTHEW. That's why you have to keep them…

SHEENA. Moist.

ADAM *exits to the sitting room.* MATTHEW *and* SHEENA *swap back the wine and mince pie.*

MATTHEW. So what did you do? Tell me.

SHEENA (*drinking, creating distance*). No, I've said too much, you'll only end up resenting me.

MATTHEW. What? Resent you? Don't be *ridunkulous*! I could *never* resent you!

SHEENA. I just wish someone else would talk to him. I wish someone would ask him what the hell is going on, because it's just me, you know, I'm by myself here.

MATTHEW. Shay, I don't know if I can be the one to…

SHEENA (*drinking*). Oh no, no, I'd never ask you to do it, he's your brother. I just feel bad for him that he can't talk to you like I do because you're such an amazing listener.

MATTHEW (*sitting, eating*). I just… try to be myself.

SHEENA. I've no idea what it's like to be married to a man like that.

Beat.

MATTHEW (*standing*). I'll talk to him for you.

SHEENA. You will? Oh thank you, thank you so much, you're wonderful.

She hugs him.

MATTHEW. Oh hey, of course, of course. I'm here for you, Okay, I'm here for you.

SHEENA (*attempting to disengage*). Thank you.

MATTHEW (*pulling her back in*). Any time. You just. Any time. Awww…

CARRIE *enters and catches them mid-hug.*

CARRIE (*standing*). Have I just walked into a parallel universe? That's *my* boyfriend. Sheena, I think you need your eyes checked!

MATTHEW. Hey… Carrie.

SHEENA. Carrie, we were just… Excuse me, I'm just going to check on Emma.

SHEENA *exits.*

CARRIE (*sitting*). What was that about?

MATTHEW. What? What d'you mean? Weren't you listening to a word she said before? Her daughter's really sick. Don't you think she might be a little bit upset? Then you tell her she needs *her eyes checked* – nice one, Carrie.

CARRIE. I was only joking. (*Standing*.) I didn't expect to walk in here and see you locked in an intimate embrace with another woman!

MATTHEW. What? What are you talking about? Are you suggesting that, that she and I are, are…?

CARRIE (*sitting*). Well I wasn't, but now I am.

MATTHEW. Carrie, don't be disgusting… (*Sitting, eating*.) She's like a big sister to me, that's how it's always been. (*Standing*.) Every time Dad missed a play or concert she'd be there cheering in the front row. And when Dad didn't come home for Christmas one year because he was with that woman from… We didn't know what to do – Mum was practically in tears the whole day. And Sheena, she, she cooked dinner, she wrapped everyone's presents, she made us do karaoke. She, she…

CARRIE. Oh my God… Do you find her attractive?

MATTHEW. What?

CARRIE. Be honest with me.

MATTHEW (*remaining standing*). Carrie, my niece is sick in bed, my father is sick in hospital, my mum's about to burst an absolute vein – what I need from you right now is a little compassion and understanding. This isn't backstage at the theatre, this is my family Christmas, yet you seem determined to make it all about you.

CARRIE. I…

MATTHEW (*sitting, eating*). I don't know what to say to you any more. This is such a ridiculous anxiety. I'm really trying to be patient, but at the end of the day, I can't keep mollycoddling you like this… (*Standing*.) Are you my partner or are you my child?

Scene Eight

The following rules are disclosed to the audience for the duration of the scene:

Rule 1: Matthew must sit and eat to tell a lie

Rule 2: Carrie must stand **and dance around** to tell a joke

Rule 3: Sheena must drink to contradict

Rule 4. Adam must affect an accent to mock

Rule 5. Edith must clean to keep calm

'Dance around' need not mean specifically to dance in the musical sense, but generally to move around, gesticulate and own the space around her.

CARRIE (*remaining seated*). Oh God… I'm sorry, you're probably right. I have been selfish. Please don't be mad at me. From now on I'm going to be completely here for you, all of you.

MATTHEW. Carrie, you don't need –

CARRIE (*standing, dancing around*). If there's one thing your family needs right now it's a maximum dose of the old Christmas Cheer, and from now on I'm bringing it one hundred – and fifty – two hundred – ten hundred per cent! I'll be Edith's Christmas helper!

EDITH *enters; she carries an ironed shirt on a hanger.*

EDITH. Did I hear my name?

CARRIE (*remaining standing and dancing around*). Edie's back! Edie, I *needie* a new job! Tell me what you want – anything. If you want me to go and get mistletoe from the wilds of Siberia, I'll fetch it. If you need me to lasso a Canadian moose for your festive garden display, I'm your gal –

MATTHEW (*ducking out the way of* CARRIE*'s exuberant gestures*). Careful, sweetie –

CARRIE. If it needs dusting, sweeping, polishing, scrubbing, I'll be your little festive…

In her exuberance, CARRIE *accidently thwacks an antique. It falls to the ground and smashes.*

Fuck!

EDITH. Oh no!

CARRIE (*sitting*). Oh my God.

MATTHEW. Oh Mum, oh dear…

CARRIE. Edith, I'm so, so sorry…! Was it an antique?

EDITH (*cleaning*). It was my father's, but don't worry, it's not important. We place too much significance on material things.

MATTHEW. Mum, let me do that, you'll cut yourself. Mum, don't clean it up, let me do it.

MATTHEW *stops* EDITH *from cleaning. Unable to clean, she is unable to keep calm.*

EDITH (*without cleaning, without calm*). No, no, leave it, *leave it* – you're mixing up the pieces! This was one of the few things my father gave to me, do you understand that, he left very little behind!

MATTHEW *releases it.* EDITH *resumes cleaning.*

CARRIE (*remaining seated*). I'm so sorry, I'm such an idiot.

MATTHEW. Hey, don't be so hard on yourself. These things happen.

ADAM *enters.*

ADAM (*affecting an accent*). Kicked off already? Did somebody lock Matthew out of the pie cupboard?

EDITH (*tidying, keeping calm*). Adam, darling, here: I've ironed one of Dad's shirts for you. And, boys, could you please finish decorating the tree? Carrie, can you cut me some thyme from the herb garden? You know what thyme looks like?

CARRIE. Yes, it's… green?

MATTHEW. I'll come with you.

EDITH (*to* MATTHEW). Fine, but then help Adam with the tree. I'm just going to finish up next door.

CARRIE. Why don't I come with you instead?

EDITH. No. Go with Matthew – you've never seen the garden before.

CARRIE. Edith, please let me help you. I feel wretched about the… thing.

EDITH. Well, that's very kind of you. Thank you.

CARRIE. And to cheer us up we can sing carols while we do it.

EDITH. Oh well, won't that be… lovely.

CARRIE (*standing, dancing around*). We three Kings of Orient are. One in a taxi, one in car. One on a scooter blowing his hooter, smoking a big cigar! Oh, star of wonder…!

EDITH *and* CARRIE *exit to the corridor;* MATTHEW *exits to the garden.*

ADAM *dresses in the shirt.* SHEENA *enters. She averts her eyes while* ADAM *hurries to dress.*

SHEENA/ADAM. Adam, I just wanted – / Look, Sheena, I'm –

SHEENA. Sorry…

ADAM. No, I'm sorry.

SHEENA. You go.

ADAM. No, you first.

SHEENA. I just wanted to say, it was a good idea to stay the night. I shouldn't have resisted.

ADAM. No, I should've asked you first. We'll leave just as soon as we've taken Emma up the hill.

SHEENA. She just told me she doesn't want to.

ADAM. What…?

SHEENA. She's afraid she won't make it to the top and doesn't want to disappoint herself. I couldn't change her mind. She said her 'decision was final'.

They share a sad smile.

ADAM. We can try and take her for a walk once we get home.

SHEENA. So… you're coming home, then?

ADAM. Yes, of course I'm coming home. I've missed you.

SHEENA. I've missed you, too.

They smile.

ADAM. Come here…

SHEENA *approaches and adjust his shirt collar.*

SHEENA. You look good in a shirt. Even an old man's shirt.

ADAM. I'm glad it looks good, cos it smells like Toilet Duck.

SHEENA (*smelling the shirt*). It does, what does she use to clean it?

ADAM. Knowing Mum, napalm.

They share a smile, she tries to get away from the smell, he pulls her into a kiss.

SHEENA. So I'll make an appointment, then. We'll get started straight away.

ADAM. Start what?

SHEENA. Couples' therapy.

ADAM (*disengaging*). What? No, no, Shay, you know exactly how I feel about couples' therapy, that's not going to change. I thought I made myself clear about that.

SHEENA *pours herself a glass of wine.*

You selectively remember conversations, we've been over this. Please don't make me repeat myself again. Let's just try and have a good day today, okay?

SHEENA. I think there's been a misunderstanding…
(*Drinking.*) You're going straight back to the Travelodge unless you agree to therapy. I made myself clear about that.

ADAM. Look, can we please talk about this when we get home. Sheena?

SHEENA (*drinking*). No, we can talk about this now and then you can come home.

ADAM. I can't talk about this now – we're in the middle of Christmas.

SHEENA. Fine, in that case you'd better do your washing overnight because you're going straight back to the hotel tomorrow.

ADAM. What kind of woman makes her husband live in a Travelodge when his father's ill in hospital?

SHEENA. I'm sorry that your father's ill… (*Drinking.*) But that doesn't change anything. I'm not going to welcome you back with open arms just because your dad's had a minor setback.

ADAM (*affecting an accent*). Stop, please, I'm drowning in sympathy.

SHEENA (*drinking*). No, you don't get to paint me as the 'bad guy' here, you're the one using your dad's illness as a 'Get Out of Jail Free' card. D'you know, I really thought this time might be different. But here you go again making excuses.

ADAM. This time *is* different, I've given a lot of thought to what you said.

SHEENA. Did you read the Information Pack?

ADAM. What Information Pack?

SHEENA (*retrieving it from her handbag*). The Information Pack the therapist gave us, the Information Pack which I photocopied and put on top of the suitcase I packed for you. Did you read it?

ADAM. Yes.

SHEENA. You did?

ADAM. Yes.

SHEENA. And?

ADAM. It made a lot of things much clearer.

SHEENA. What things did it make clearer?

ADAM. Just the… mechanism… of the whole… process… I read the first couple of pages.

SHEENA. You read the first couple of pages.

ADAM. And that was enough. Look, with all due respect, it was the biggest load of pseudo-psychological nonsense I'd ever read in my life.

Scene Nine

The following rules are disclosed to the audience for the duration of the scene:

Rule 1: Matthew must sit and eat to tell a lie

Rule 2: Carrie must stand and dance around to tell a joke

Rule 3: Sheena must drink **and interrupt** to contradict

Rule 4. Adam must affect an accent to mock

Rule 5. Edith must clean to keep calm

A slash (/) marks the point where SHEENA *interrupts the preceding person's speech.*

ADAM (*affecting an accent, mocking the Information Pack*). 'Robbie's mother never told him she loved him and so now he's addicted to sex with strangers. Selena's sister was always getting better grades / than her so now she feels inadequate – '

SHEENA (*drinking, interrupting*). No, no, don't you dare mock me.

ADAM. I'm not mocking you, I'm mocking the pamphlet / you are wilfully misunderstanding me as usual.

SHEENA (*drinking, interrupting*). Yes, you are, it's implied, it's always implied. This is how we're helping our daughter, Adam – are you saying you don't want our daughter getting help?

ADAM. Of course I want Emma to get whatever help she needs. I'm just saying we don't need to subject ourselves to this as well, when it's really only Emma who's got a problem / we can just –

SHEENA (*drinking, interrupting*). It is *not* just Emma who's got a problem. Our behaviour, our marriage, is affecting our child. And until you're prepared to admit that – until you're prepared to take our marriage seriously – then you can stay in a hotel.

ADAM. Of course I take our marriage seriously, that's why I've got no interest in letting a complete stranger tell us what to do with it, and charge me a hundred pounds an hour for the privilege. / Some of us value our privacy.

SHEENA (*drinking, interrupting*). It's not a hundred pounds an hour, it's not a hundred pounds an hour, it's *eighty* pounds an hour, which I consider pretty good value if it saves your marriage.

ADAM. Therapy isn't going to magically fix everything. / People have therapy all the time and it doesn't change anything.

SHEENA (*drinking, interrupting*). Well it's a start, it's a start, it's a start!

ADAM. Keep your voice down. (*Beat.*) Let me ask you something, do you really think / the two of us being lectured by some bearded –

SHEENA (*drinking, interruption*). No, you need to listen to me –

ADAM. Can I ask you something, / or is nobody else allowed to talk?

SHEENA (*drinking, interrupting*). No, no, you need to listen to me and hear me.

ADAM. I've heard you: you want us to change. And we can change. / We can deal with it ourselves.

SHEENA (*drinking, interrupting*). No, no we can't, we say we will and it changes for two weeks and then it goes back to normal – or worse, you throw away your opportunity at partnership –

> ADAM *goes in search of his cigarettes,* SHEENA *hounds him.*

– all you had to do was wear an ironed shirt and take the right people to dinner, but you didn't, you didn't do it.

ADAM. I told you, I am not a hack.

SHEENA. Yes, I know, you didn't want to be 'a hack', but I don't think that's what it was about. Because it's not just the job, it's our anniversary, it's the tree house that's still in the box in the garage. It's the 5K run you signed up for but never trained for, it's the book on sexual intimacy you claim you read, but clearly haven't, it's everything you say you'll try but never do. Maybe that's your 'rule' – you never see anything through!

Scene Ten

The following rules are disclosed to the audience for the duration of the scene:

Rule 1: Matthew must sit and eat to tell a lie

Rule 2: Carrie must stand and dance around to tell a joke

Rule 3: Sheena must drink and interrupt to contradict

Rule 4. Adam must affect an accent **and name-call** to mock

Rule 5. Edith must clean to keep calm

ADAM. Look… I know you so badly want me to fit your little model, but, honey, / not everybody –

SHEENA (*drinking, interrupting*). Don't call me honey.

ADAM (*affecting an accent*). Okay, Dr Psychobabble, one size doesn't fit all – we're not cardboard cut-outs, we're human beings / and we're just not that predictable.

SHEENA (*drinking, interrupting*). But how would you know unless you made the effort to find out?

ADAM (*affecting an accent*). I'm sorry I'm not the perfect spinach-juicing, yogurt-knitting yoga-bunny like you, but I don't believe everything I see on daytime television, / okay, Captain Credulous?

SHEENA (*drinking, interrupting*). Or in medical journals, in medical journals – where are you going?

ADAM. You clearly want to be the only person involved in this conversation, so I'm going to luxuriate in a cigarette in the car and you can fill in the gaps however you like.

SHEENA. Sure, have another cigarette, and add 'cutting back' to the list of things you never do.

ADAM (*affecting an accent*). That's rich coming from the old souse – what happened to pacing yourself? / How many glasses is that?

SHEENA (*drinking, interrupting*). I am pacing myself, I've had *one* drink. I think it's safe to have one glass of wine when the meal is going to be pretty substantive.

ADAM (*affecting an accent*). Substantial, Clogs. The meal is going to be pretty *substantial*.

SHEENA. Look, you begged me to come here, I'm here. You want me to pretend we have a functioning marriage, I'm pretending. But while I do all that, I think it's fair enough to have *one* bloody glass of wine!

EDITH *enters.* SHEENA *and* ADAM *immediately assume the pose of a happy couple.*

EDITH. Oh, look at you two: still canoodling in the kitchen like you did as teenagers. That takes me back. Where is that brother of yours, is he still out in the – ?

EDITH *opens the back door to call out to* MATTHEW, *but he is standing in the doorway.*

Oh, Matthew! You gave me a fright.

MATTHEW (*entering, carrying the thyme*). Hi, Mum.

SHEENA *and* ADAM *share a look – has he been there all along listening to their conversation?*

ADAM. How long have you been standing there?

MATTHEW (*sitting, eating the thyme*). Not long… I just… got there. There's a frost, it was hard to cut.

EDITH (*referring to the food*). Hands off, no picking, you'll spoil your appetite. Now how are we all getting on with our jobs? (*Returning to her list, crossing off items.*) Adam's made a fire. Sheena's tasted the wine… and helped herself to a glass, how nice. Carrie's hoovering the stairs.

MATTHEW (*standing*). Are you all right with her, Mum, is she helping you? I know she can be a bit much sometimes.

EDITH (*cleaning*). She's certainly enthusiastic, I understand why she's a performer. Does it run in the family?

MATTHEW. Her sister's a ballet dancer. You've heard of her: Rosie Reynolds. She played Juliet for the Royal Ballet last year.

EDITH. No, that's Carrie's sister? She was magnificent, like a swan. Oh, well, that explains a lot, then.

MATTHEW. What d'you mean?

CARRIE *enters, standing, dancing around and belting out a show tune.*

CARRIE (*sitting*). Sorry, I get rather overexcited at Christmas. It's my favourite holiday.

ADAM (*affecting an accent*). Mine too, Barbie!

CARRIE. Barbie?

ADAM (*affecting an accent*). What's not to love about an appropriated pagan festival?

EDITH. Adam…

ADAM (*affecting an accent*). Assorted sausages in bacon are an entirely appropriate way of celebrating the fake birthday of a Middle Eastern Jewish radical, aren't they, Matron?

EDITH (*cleaning*). Now, Adam, if you have nothing nice to say, please say nothing at all. (*Thrusting an envelope at him.*) Now look, before I forget: we haven't done you a main present this year, but Dad's written you each a cheque. (*Handing the others round.*) Please don't forget to thank him, I think he's been more than generous.

MATTHEW. Mum, we've got you something pretty special this year, haven't we? We've been secretly hatching a plan, and we've got you a joint gift this year.

EDITH. You have? Oh darlings, how sweet of you. Where is it, is it under the tree?

SHEENA. Where is it, Matt, I can't see it?

MATTHEW. I don't know, where did you put it?

SHEENA. I didn't put it anywhere, you brought it.

MATTHEW. No… you were supposed to bring it. / You said you'd pick it up on your –

SHEENA (*drinking, interrupting*). No, no, no, I specifically said I couldn't because of Emma.

MATTHEW. I said I couldn't get away from work, and Carrie was with her parents.

MATTHEW/CARRIE. Oh no…! / Oh God…

SHEENA. How could we be so stupid?

EDITH. You didn't get me a Christmas present, then?

MATTHEW. No, no we did.

CARRIE. We've been planning it for ages.

SHEENA. We just appear to have… forgotten it.

Scene Eleven

The following rules are disclosed to the audience for the duration of the scene:

Rule 1: Matthew must sit and eat to tell a lie

Rule 2: Carrie must stand and dance around to tell a joke

Rule 3: Sheena must drink and interrupt to contradict

Rule 4. Adam must affect an accent and name-call to mock

Rule 5. Edith must clean and **self-medicate** to keep calm

MATTHEW (*remaining standing*). Mum, I'm so sorry…

ADAM. We're really sorry, Mum…

> EDITH *retrieves a sachet of soluble pain medication. She mixes it in a glass of water. She cleans up after herself as she goes, and takes a drink as soon as it's ready.*

SHEENA. As soon as we get home we'll post it.

CARRIE (*remaining seated*). We'll courier it.

MATTHEW. I'll drive it up in the car just as soon as I get home.

EDITH (*continuing to clean*). Oh it doesn't matter in the slightest. Mums don't need presents. Christmas is about the children. Besides I always buy a spare present in case of emergencies. And actually when I bought them I thought to myself, I'd really rather like these coffee spoons, so I'm very glad I get to keep them.

> EDITH *drinks another sip of medicine and continues to clean.*

MATTHEW. Mum, what's that you're drinking?

EDITH (*cleaning*). Now come on, everyone get on with your jobs. We're really up against it.

ADAM. Look, Mum… Mum…? We wanted it to be a surprise, but we might as well tell you. You know the antique games compendium Grandfather gave you.

MATTHEW. The one we basically pillaged and ruined over the years.

EDITH (*cleaning, sipping medicine*). Daddy's games box?

ADAM. Between us we concocted a plan to restore it. Matthew took it last time he was here.

MATTHEW. Why d'you think I brought a suitcase to stay one night?

ADAM. We've been going backwards and forwards, trying to choose the right pieces.

MATTHEW. A new set of wooden drafts.

SHEENA. He's repainted the cribbage board.

CARRIE. And there's a dice-shaker thingy.

EDITH (*cleaning, sipping medicine*). Oh darlings, Dad'll be so impressed with all the trouble you've gone to for us.

ADAM. We did it for you, Mum.

EDITH (*cleaning, sipping medicine*). Now, boys, you need to make headway with the tree. Carrie, could you give the upstairs loo a once-over; I'll do the downstairs loo?

CARRIE (*standing, dancing around*). Sure thing: just call me Mr Muscle. Mrs Muscle. Oh, I'm unmarried: *Ms* Muscle!

EDITH *returns for her glass of medicine before exiting alongside* CARRIE.

SHEENA. I'll just check on Emma.

SHEENA *signals to* MATTHEW *that now would be a good time to talk to* ADAM, *then exits*.

ADAM. Come on then, let's get this over with.

They begin decorating the Christmas tree.

ADAM *lifts two home-made Christmas angels out of a box.*

Hello… I remember you two. I think you made this one?

MATTHEW. No that one's yours – I remember the ears.

ADAM. Those are wings.

MATTHEW. Dad's annual competition – (*Impersonating* FRANCIS.) 'Who gets their angel on top of the tree?'

ADAM (*impersonating* FRANCIS). 'Best son wins.' (*Beat.*) Divide and rule. Classic military tactics.

MATTHEW. It's more of a governance.

ADAM. Shut up, Matthew.

MATTHEW. Tactic. Dad was wasted as a judge. He should've been in the army.

ADAM (*affecting an accent*). Why do you think I call him 'The General'? (*Impersonating* FRANCIS.) 'There can be only one winner. Because that, my boys, is how real life works, so you better get used to it.'

They laugh, a little uncomfortably.

At least we don't have to worry about that any more. You know… the two of us, competing… for one indivisible prize.

MATTHEW. Exactly.

ADAM. Yeah.

Pause.

MATTHEW. So… (*Unwrapping a chocolate Christmas tree decoration.*) How are things with you and Sheena?

ADAM. Yeah. Everything's great.

MATTHEW. Really? I got a sense there was… trouble in paradise.

ADAM. You've got the sixth sense have you?

MATTHEW. No, no I just mean that I'm picking up some strange vibes that's all.

ADAM. Are you picking up strange vibes or are you picking up the telephone?

MATTHEW. What…?

ADAM. Why d'you call Sheena when I'm not around?

MATTHEW (*sitting, eating*). I don't call Sheena when you're not around.

ADAM. Why d'you need to call her at all?

MATTHEW (*standing to reach another chocolate decoration*). Because… because she's my friend.

ADAM (*affecting an accent*). So you're just two friends, talking on the phone, twice a week, for two hours at a time. What are you, a teenage girl, Doris Day?

MATTHEW (*standing*). No, I'm not a teenage girl.

ADAM (*affecting an accent*). Then what are you doing, Doris?

MATTHEW. Please don't call me Doris, you know I don't like being called Doris.

ADAM (*affecting an accent*). What are you trying to do, Judy Garland?

CARRIE *enters, unseen by* MATTHEW *or* ADAM.

MATTHEW (*sitting, eating*). I'm not trying to do anything. I'm just trying to support Sheena.

ADAM. Support her?

MATTHEW (*remaining seated, eating*). Yes.

ADAM. Are you trying to support Sheena or seduce her?

Beat.

CARRIE (*sitting*). What the hell does that mean?

The phone rings, shrilly. EDITH *bursts into the room, carrying her glass of medicine.*

EDITH. I'll get it, I'll get it…! (*Answering the phone.*)… four–seven–five–six–four–two Edith speaking… Yes, hello, Karen… Happy Christmas to you, too. What!

CARRIE. Matthew…?

MATTHEW. Shhh…

EDITH *takes a gulp of medicine and begins cleaning.*

EDITH (*cleaning*). Oh right, right, well that's unexpected…
No, no, that's fine, sure, that's absolutely fine… All right,
great, lovely, bye then.

EDITH *hangs up the phone, takes another sip of medicine
and continues cleaning.*

(*Cleaning, with calm.*) Right, nobody panic, but… It's Dad,
he's early, they're just turning off the main road.

MATTHEW. What…?

EDITH (*cleaning, sipping medicine*). Yes, but it's not a
problem. It's absolutely not a problem. In fact, it's lovely to
have him with us sooner than we thought. Isn't it?

MATTHEW (*sitting, eating*). Oh yeah, it's great.

ADAM. Yeah, great, brilliant.

MATTHEW (*sitting, eating*). Brilliant news!

EDITH (*cleaning*). Quickly, quickly you have to stop what
you're doing and tidy up. Adam, darling, why don't you get
the champagne out of the fridge. Carrie, would you lay out
the flutes – they're in the cabinet.

CARRIE. Actually, Matthew, can I just have a quick word
upstairs?

EDITH (*cleaning*). Carrie, darling, we don't have time so could
you just please do as I asked?

SHEENA *enters.*

(*Cleaning.*) There you are. Francis is about two minutes
away.

SHEENA. What?

EDITH (*cleaning*). It's not a problem, but I need you to help
Carrie with the glasses, please?

SHEENA. Sure, I just need Matthew's help upstairs for a
moment.

EDITH (*cleaning*). No, I'm sorry, there isn't time.

CARRIE. Actually Matt's just having a word with me.

ADAM. Matt, why don't we step outside for a minute?

EDITH puts down her glass of medicine and stops cleaning.

EDITH (*without cleaning, without calm*). No, no, absolutely not. Nobody is going anywhere. I'm not having your father arrive to an empty room. That is out of the question. We're going to stay in here and welcome him as a family. We're going to have a glass of bubbly and calmly catch him up with our news, we're going to play a game, like we always do, and then we are going to sit down as a family to our Christmas meal, and we are going to give him our time and attention, and show him the respect he deserves.

The doorbell rings.

ADAM. I'll go.

MATTHEW. I'll get it.

EDITH (*without cleaning, without calm*). I'll go. Now you know the deal: his roof, his rules. No muddy shoes in the house. No electronics at the table. No smoking. No swearing. No talking with your mouth full. The following topics of conversation are out of bounds: illness, dietary requirements, therapy, politics, religion, divorce, sex, death and global warming.

ADAM. Then what are we going to talk about?

EDITH. I'm sure you'll think of something, and if you can't, follow the golden rule which is, my darlings, that if you have nothing nice to say you will say nothing at all! (*Taking a sip of medicine, calling out with renewed calm.*) Coming!

EDITH exits.

The others arrange themselves into position. They adjust their appearances. They wait in tense silence. The door opens. EDITH enters pushing FRANCIS in a wheelchair.

Here they are, here they are!

MATTHEW/ADAM. Hi, Dad. / Happy Christmas, Dad!

EDITH. There they are, everybody's here! You've arrived.

The brothers move to help their mother with the wheelchair.

Mind the step. Matthew, mind the step.

MATTHEW. I'm minding the step.

EDITH. Don't crowd him, Matthew, let Adam do it. To the left a bit. Left. In you come, in you come.

SHEENA. Happy Christmas, Francis!

CARRIE. Happy Christmas!

EDITH. Let him get in the door, first. Wait a minute. There we go, over there. Give him some space, give him some space. There we go. Here we are. Come on, boys. Come and say hello to your dad.

ADAM. Hi, Dad, it's great to see you, how are you feeling?

MATTHEW. Hey, Dad, welcome home, how are you?

FRANCIS attempts to speak with great difficulty.

ADAM. Sorry… I… what was that, Dad? Mum, I don't understand what he's saying.

They all stare at him in shocked silence: this is far worse than they expected.

EDITH *reaches for her glass of medicine.*

Mum…?

EDITH (*draining her glass of medicine*). Darling, isn't it obvious? He's saying 'Happy Christmas!' of course!

ACT TWO

Scene One

The following rules are displayed to the audience for the duration of the scene:

Rule 1: Matthew must sit and eat to tell a lie

Rule 2: Carrie must stand and dance around to tell a joke

Rule 3: Sheena must drink and interrupt to contradict

Rule 4. Adam must affect an accent and name-call to mock

Rule 5. Edith must clean and self-medicate to keep calm

We return to the family exactly as we left them at the end of Act One. No time has passed.

FRANCIS *has suffered a post-operative stroke. As a result he is suffering from right-sided partial paralysis, and expressive (non-fluent) aphasia – a loss of his ability to produce language. He is only able to say simple words and phrases, not complete sentences, and struggles to make even those words understood.*

EDITH. Darling, isn't it obvious? He's saying 'Happy Christmas!' of course.

ALL. Happy Christmas.

    FRANCIS *reaches out to* SHEENA *and tries to say her name.*

EDITH (*translating for* FRANCIS). Sheena? Yes, Sheena's here. I told you she'd be here.

SHEENA. Hello, Francis… Happy Christmas.

EDITH. Francis, you remember me telling you about Carrie, don't you? Matthew's girlfriend.

CARRIE (*standing, dancing around*). Don't get up...! (*Sitting*.) Hello, Francis, it's lovely to meet you.

SHEENA. I'm sorry, I can't hear what you're...

EDITH (*translating*). Champagne! Yes, of course! Adam, my darling, would you do the honours?

ADAM. Mum, what's happened...?

EDITH *retrieves a second sachet of soluble pain medication and begins to mix it in a glass of water. She cleans up as she goes, and takes a sip as soon as it's ready. She sips medicine routinely as and when she needs calming.*

EDITH. Oh it's that horrid tube-thing they put down his throat – the doctor said the inflammation goes away eventually. There's orange juice if anybody wants to make a Buck's Fizz. Sheena?

MATTHEW. Can... can he understand us?

EDITH. Of course he can; you can understand everything, can't you, Francis? Now stop making a fuss and let's have a glass of champagne.

ADAM. But, Mum, he can hardly move his... what's the matter with...?

EDITH. Adam, your father doesn't want questions about his health. He wants to get on with Christmas.

EDITH *takes a swig of medicine, and begins to clean a beaker for* FRANCIS.

You're in for a treat, Francis, we've spared no expense: turkey with *all* the trimmings. Matthew's brought an intriguing new game for us to play...

FRANCIS *rejects the beaker.*

What, a glass? But this has a handle like the one – ? No, okay, all right... (*Fetching and cleaning a champagne glass for* FRANCIS.) Look at us all, standing around. Matthew, Adam, sit down with your dad. Tell him how you are. Adam, go on, tell your father.

EDITH *offers* FRANCIS *a glass of champagne with a straw.*
He determines to remove the straw.

ADAM. I'm good, Dad…

FRANCIS *tries to engage* ADAM *in conversation about his*
cricket practice, but the only words he is able to articulate
are 'bat', 'ball' and 'line'.

Things are looking good at the firm. We… what's that? Is
that… ball? Is that cricket? Mum, I don't…?

EDITH (*translating*). What's that, Francis? Oh yes, yes – line
and length.

ADAM. Line and length? Yeah… 'line and length' I remember
you telling me. Dad was always full of advice about the
cricket. That didn't work out so well for me though, did it?

FRANCIS *becomes confused.*

I don't play cricket any more. I haven't played for years. I'm
a solicitor now. You know that…

FRANCIS *becomes frustrated.*

EDITH. Francis, Matthew has some wonderful news. Matthew,
tell Dad your big news. Matthew?

MATTHEW. I… I've been offered partnership by the firm.

EDITH. Isn't that fantastic? Astonishing.

FRANCIS *tries to speak – he wants to talk about*
MATTHEW*'s performance as the Major General, but the*
only word he is able to articulate is 'Major'.

MATTHEW. What's that, Dad…? I can't…

EDITH (*translating*). Major…? Oh yes, Major General.

MATTHEW. Major General…?

EDITH. He was wonderful in the *Pirates of Penzance*, wasn't
he? Do a bit for your dad. Go on.

MATTHEW. No, I don't sing any more. I gave that up a long
time ago.

FRANCIS *becomes confused and upset.*

I'm a solicitor now, Dad.

FRANCIS *becomes frustrated and angry.*

EDITH. It's all right, darling. I know, it's confusing.

ADAM. Mum, what's happening?

EDITH *takes a good gulp of pain medication.*

EDITH (*cleaning*). Sometimes he gets confused and I find that if you correct him, it's all the more upsetting. Apparently it's fairly common after a setback of this kind.

ADAM. What kind? What exactly did the doctor say? What were his exact words?

EDITH (*cleaning*). He said it's called a 'delayed... stroke'.

ADAM. What!

MATTHEW. A stroke!

SHEENA. Oh my God...

EDITH (*sipping medicine, cleaning*). A *minor* stroke, a very minor, very common side affect of cardiac surgery and most people fully recover.

ADAM. How could you not tell us about this?

EDITH. I didn't want to worry you over nothing. (*To* FRANCIS, *cleaning him.*) Darling, I'm sorry, talking about you as if you're not there – how rude of us.

ADAM. We need to talk to a doctor –

EDITH (*cleaning, sipping medicine*). It's Christmas, there are no doctors to talk to. And it won't do any good to cause a scene. He's on some very strong pain medication, and for now, he remembers what he remembers –

ADAM. Which is what?

EDITH. Well, clearly he still thinks that his youngest son acts and you still...

ADAM. Play cricket.

EDITH (*cleaning*). Yes. And I'd be very grateful if you would please…

MATTHEW. Play along.

EDITH (*cleaning*). It's only temporary.

ADAM. But, Mum, this is –

EDITH (*cleaning, sipping medication*). Darling, it's Christmas. (*Beat.*) Adam, talk to your father about practice, he's keen to know. Adam?

ADAM. Things are good, Dad… I'm working on my line and length…

FRANCIS *manages to articulate the word 'fast'.*

I was always a very – sorry, I *am* a very fast bowler. But Dad thinks I need to work on my 'line and length'. Like Glen McGrath.

CARRIE (*remaining seated*). Who's Glen McGrath?

ADAM (*affecting an accent*). Did they teach you nothing at drama school, Barbie?

MATTHEW. He's a bowler.

ADAM (*affecting an accent*). The most economical bowler of all time because of the accuracy and consistency of his *line and length* – his aim. Dad wants me to bowl like Glen McGrath. Isn't that right, sir? General, sir!

FRANCIS *tries to encourage his son – he is able to say 'good boy'.*

EDITH (*translating*). Yes, that's right. He can do anything he puts his mind to. He's a real talent.

Beat.

ADAM. Matt, why don't you sing for Dad?

MATTHEW. I'll sing it later.

FRANCIS *tries to insist, but the only word he can say is 'Major'.*

EDITH. Oh yes, sing a bit for Dad.

ADAM (*affecting an accent*). Go on, Michael Ball, don't deny him. Give us a song.

> MATTHEW *half-heartedly sings the first verse and chorus of the Major General's Song from Gilbert & Sullivan's* The Pirates of Penzance. CARRIE *watches the scene unfold with disbelief.*

MATTHEW (*standing, singing*).
> I am the very model of a modern Major-General,
> I've information vegetable, animal, and mineral,
> I know the kings of England, and I quote the fights
>   historical,
> From Marathon to Waterloo, in order categorical,
> I'm very well acquainted, too, with matters mathematical,
> I understand equations, both the simple and quadratical,
> About binomial theorem I'm teeming with a lot o' news,
> With many cheerful facts about the square of the
>   hypotenuse.

EDITH. Don't stop, keep going.

MATTHEW (*singing*).
> I'm very good at integral and differential calculus…
> I know the scientific names of beings animalculous:
> In short, in matters vegetable, animal and mineral,
> I am the very model of a modern Major-General!

> *They all applaud.*

ADAM (*affecting an accent*). As good today as it was then, Barbra Streisand.

MATTHEW. Bit like your bowling, mate.

EDITH. Now who'd like a mince pie?

ADAM (*affecting an accent*). Perhaps you needed to do your vocal warm-up, Pavarotti.

EDITH. We've got two sorts: one from Sheena and the other made by Carrie.

ADAM. Me ma me ma me ma me ma… rrrrrrr… Double bubble gum, quadruple double bubble gum… I've got a tiny little –

MATTHEW. Hey, Adam, maybe you need to go outside and practise your line and length? Why don't we all come out and watch you? We could set out some chairs, put up a scoreboard?

FRANCIS *attempts to intervene as his sons bicker. He's frustrated by his inability to control them.*

EDITH. Speaking of scoreboards, why don't we play a game?

SHEENA. I'll try one of Carrie's.

ADAM (*affecting an accent*). When I'm a famous movie star I'm going to buy my mummy a house and my daddy a house, but not my *stinky brother*. No house for you!

CARRIE. I'll have one of Sheena's.

MATTHEW (*imitating his fourteen-year-old brother*). When I'm Captain of the England team I'm going to have six girlfriends and a Ferrari.

SHEENA. Mmm, Carrie, how do you get such a… crunch?

ADAM (*affecting an accent*). When I leave school I'm going to go to RADA because that's where all the best most famous actors go.

CARRIE. Sheena, these are… you just don't need the sugar, do you?

MATTHEW. When I'm a sports star I'm going to be even more famous than my *daddy*.

ADAM (*affecting an accent*). I hope I don't let my daddy talk me out of it and end up at law school instead of drama school.

MATTHEW. I hope I don't completely lose my nerve in front of thousands of people and fail ever again to get it back.

EDITH. Matthew, Adam, I need a hand with the card table, please.

ADAM (*affecting an accent*). Because acting's just a hobby, isn't that right, General? Definitely not a viable career option! No, sir!

MATTHEW (*imitating* ADAM). My arm! My arm! (*Clumsily bowling an imaginary ball*.) What's happening! Every time I bowl the ball I just keep punching myself in the face!

EDITH *cries out in pain and clutches her back.*

Mum – ! (*Attending to his mother*.) Mum, stop it, you're overdoing it.

EDITH *retrieves a third sachet of pain medication and begins to mix it with water.*

EDITH (*attempting to clean*). I'm not overdoing it.

MATTHEW. We're not having you on your back for days like last time. What is that?

EDITH. It's just Solpadine. Go and set up your game, please.

MATTHEW *inspects the dosage instructions on the packet.*

MATTHEW. Yeah, but you're not supposed to drink it like orange squash.

EDITH (*attempting to clean*). Don't fuss, don't fuss.

MATTHEW (*confiscating the medication*). No, Mum, that's enough, you've had two already.

MATTHEW *prevents* EDITH *from self-medicating.* EDITH *is unable to keep calm.*

EDITH (*without cleaning, without calm*). Stop manhandling me! Why do you have to always fuss around me? Wherever I am you're always there invading my space. You were the same as child, clinging to my skirts, desperate to please, desperate for approval!

In his frustration, FRANCIS *spills the contents of his champagne glass over himself.*

Oh look what's happened now. I'm sorry, Francis, Matthew was distracting me. Oh dear, you'll need a new shirt. Adam and Sheena, help me, please. Matthew, set up your game please, it's your responsibility. (*To* ADAM.) Careful, careful.

ADAM, SHEENA, EDITH *and* FRANCIS *exit.*

MATTHEW (*standing*). Oh my God… It's bad, isn't it? He's in a really bad way. I had no idea that he'd be this… Mum said he was recovering, he was getting better. She must be in denial. What if he doesn't get better? What if he's always…? Carrie, I think I'm in shock. Can I have a hug?

CARRIE *and* MATTHEW *hug. After a moment…*

CARRIE (*remaining seated*). Matthew, what was Adam talking about just now before Francis arrived?

MATTHEW. What?

CARRIE. Why did he accuse you of trying to seduce Sheena? I really want to be there for you – and I am – but I need to know. And before you answer, stop telling me what you think I want to hear and try telling the truth.

Scene Two

The following rules are displayed to the audience for the duration of the scene:

Rule 1: Matthew must sit and eat to tell a lie… **until he gets a compliment**

Rule 2: Carrie must stand and dance around to tell a joke

Rule 3: Sheena must drink and interrupt to contradict

Rule 4. Adam must affect an accent and name-call to mock

Rule 5. Edith must clean and self-medicate to keep calm

From now on, once MATTHEW *has started lying, he cannot stop lying until he receives a compliment. You may wish to add a sound effect or visual cue to indicate that a rule has become activated (or 'live'), and another to indicate that the rule has been deactivated (or 'no longer live').*

MATTHEW (*standing*). All right you want the truth, here's the truth: Sheena and Adam are having serious problems. And the moment I asked him about it, he just started attacking me. He's become incredibly defensive. (*Whispering*.) Ever since the cricket. It really messed with his head. But he's in total denial about it, he just wants to pretend everything's fine.

CARRIE. There seems to be a lot of that going around.

MATTHEW. What are you talking about?

CARRIE. Is there something going on between you and Sheena?

MATTHEW (*standing*). No, no of course not.

CARRIE. Do you want there to be something going on with you and Sheena?

Rule 1 becomes live. It will remain live until MATTHEW *gets a compliment.*

MATTHEW (*sitting, eating*). No, no of course I don't. I've never even contemplated it. Why would I when I'm so in love with you…? You're my perfect woman… I still feel exactly the same way about you as when we first met. Don't you feel the same?

CARRIE. I just feel… like you're pulling away from me.

Having failed to get a compliment, MATTHEW *must tell another lie.*

MATTHEW (*sitting, eating*). No, no, not at all – I still wake up every day thanking my lucky stars you're mine. Don't you…?

CARRIE. Well… then what are we doing? We've been together nearly a year and we haven't even talked about going on holiday together, yet. In fact you didn't even ask me to come with you for Christmas – I had to ask myself. And I get here and you're being accused of seducing Sheena! What am I supposed to think? I really want to believe you, but there's this nagging voice telling me that you're just stringing me along.

Having still failed to get a compliment, MATTHEW *must tell another lie.*

MATTHEW (*searching for more food*). What…? Carrie…!

CARRIE. And I don't want to waste another year of my life while you keep stalling. I mean I don't even want to waste another minute. I'm going to get my coat and go explain why I'm not staying for lunch.

MATTHEW. No, no, no… (*Finding food, sitting, eating.*) Carrie, you're being completely unreasonable.

CARRIE. Well either you're stringing me along or you're not. Actions speak louder than words.

MATTHEW (*remaining seated, eating*). I'm not, I'm not. In fact…

CARRIE. Yes?

MATTHEW (*remaining seated, eating*). I was going to…

CARRIE. What?

MATTHEW (*remaining seated, eating*). Propose.

CARRIE. What…? When…?

MATTHEW (*remaining seated, eating*). Today.

CARRIE. Are you being serious?

MATTHEW (*remaining seated, eating*). Yes.

CARRIE. Have you got a ring?

MATTHEW (*remaining seated, eating*). Yes.

CARRIE. Where is it?

MATTHEW (*remaining seated, eating*). Upstairs. That's why Sheena was hugging me – I was… asking her advice. About the best time to propose.

CARRIE. Oh my God… I can't believe it! You're going to propose? Oh God, I'm such an idiot, I'm so sorry I accused you of all those terrible things. I love you, too, you're my perfect man.

Having finally got a compliment, Rule 1 is no longer live.

MATTHEW (*standing, without eating*). Thank you.

CARRIE. Oh my God we're getting married!

MATTHEW (*remaining standing*). Oh my God we're getting married…

CARRIE. I can't believe you're going to propose!

MATTHEW. Neither can I…

CARRIE (*sitting*). I can't wait to tell your family!

MATTHEW. Wait. Wait, slow down. Honey, the thing is, the situation with my dad is a lot worse than I thought. He's already so confused. Can we wait until he's well enough to understand?

CARRIE. Of course, but… Can we at least tell your mum?

MATTHEW. Oh no, definitely not.

CARRIE. Why not, you think she won't be pleased?

MATTHEW. I… I didn't say that.

CARRIE. She doesn't like me. I knew it – she's never liked me and I'm never going to fit in!

Scene Three

The following rules are displayed to the audience for the duration of the scene:

Rule 1: Matthew must sit and eat to tell a lie… until he gets a compliment

Rule 2: Carrie must stand and dance around to tell a joke… **until she gets a laugh**

Rule 3: Sheena must drink and interrupt to contradict

Rule 4. Adam must affect an accent and name-call to mock

Rule 5. Edith must clean and self-medicate to keep calm

From now on, once CARRIE *has started joking, she cannot stop joking until she gets a laugh.*

MATTHEW. Carrie, I'm just saying Mum has a lot on her plate right now. Besides, she wouldn't be able to keep it a secret from Dad, and we need to tread carefully given the state he's in.

CARRIE. So all the more reason to tell him now, before it's too late.

MATTHEW. What? Dad's barely through the door and you're already thinking he's going to… How can you say such a thing to me?

Rule 2 becomes live; it will remain live until CARRIE *gets a laugh.*

CARRIE. I'm sorry, I didn't… Course we can keep it a secret – the only important people here are you and me… (*Standing and dancing around.*) And Beyoncé! So to paraphrase her words 'you like it so you're gonna put a ring on it'. Yes you like it so you're gonna put a ring on it!

MATTHEW. Carrie, it's not funny –

Having failed to get a laugh, CARRIE *must tell another joke.*

CARRIE (*standing, dancing around*). Oh, you won't be mad when you see that he wants it. Because you like it so you're gonna put a ring on it. Whoa oh oh oh oh oh oh oh oh oh oh ooh woh oh oh –

MATTHEW *restrains* CARRIE *and forces her to sit.*

MATTHEW. No, Carrie, this is what I'm talking about. Mum and Dad are very fragile right now – I need you to really dial it back, like all the way. Or are you physically incapable of doing that?

Having still failed to get a laugh, CARRIE *must tell another joke.*

CARRIE (*pulling out of* MATTHEW's *grip, standing, dancing around*). Er hello, have you met me? I'm physically capable of anything! High kick of subtlety!

As CARRIE *chases her laugh,* MATTHEW *chases* CARRIE *in an attempt to restrain her.*

(*Standing, dancing around.*) I can blend in. I can totes blend in. Look at me, look… (*Imitating a piece of furniture.*) What am I?… No, what am I?… No, I'm a lamp! Is that a cheese biscuit selection or is that Carrie? Nobody knows because she's so inconspicuous. Look… I'm just part of the furniture! I'm just… (*Disguising herself.*) I'm just blending right in. I'm fading into the background.

MATTHEW. Carrie, Carrie, I need you to listen to me –

CARRIE (*standing, dancing around, raising her voice*). I am listening to you – I'm *all ears*! Like a mouse, with massive ears, and you can't be cross with such a teeny, weeny, well-behaved, very quiet little mouse. Who loves you.

CARRIE *tickles* MATTHEW, *it produces a laugh.*

There it is! (*Sitting.*) Thank you very much, I'll be here all night!

Having got a laugh, Rule 2 is no longer live.

(*Remaining seated.*) Sorry, consider me 'on mute' – you won't even know I'm here.

EDITH *and* SHEENA *enter, followed by* ADAM *pushing* FRANCIS *in his wheelchair.*

EDITH. Why haven't you arranged the card table? What have you been doing, get a move on?

MATTHEW. Actually, Mum, I think this game might be a bit complicated… for Dad.

EDITH. You and Dad play on the same team. Now, let's move these aside shall we, and make a space?

ADAM. Mum, I'm not sure Dad wants to play a game.

EDITH. Of course your father wants to play a game.

ADAM. Mum, I'm not sure he *can* play a game.

FRANCIS *insists that he does want to play a game – he succeeds in articulating the word 'game'.*

EDITH. Dad is fine! This is about you: you don't like to play games because you're afraid of losing. Now stop being such a scaredy-cat – it's only a game!

Beat. SHEENA *stares at* ADAM, *the penny drops –* ADAM *is afraid of failure and so avoids risk.*

EDITH *retrieves a chewable pain-relief tablet, or lozenge. She pops one in her mouth.*

CARRIE *is sat beside* FRANCIS, *he takes her hand.*

Sheena, why don't you arrange the chairs? Sheena?

ADAM (*affecting an accent*). What are you staring at, Goggle-eyes?

SHEENA *arranges the chairs.* FRANCIS *tries to compliment* CARRIE, *but he's unable to say the words pretty, he says 'girl' instead.*

CARRIE. What's that...? I don't...?

EDITH (*cleaning, chewing her lozenge*). Yes, she does have beautiful nails, doesn't she? Not like mine, I know; that's gardening for you. If you want a garden to look like yours, Francis, someone has to do the work. Now who has the rules? Adam come here and find the instructions.

ADAM (*finding the rules*). Here they are.

EDITH. Read them out, then.

ADAM. Somebody else do it.

EDITH. Read the rules, Adam. Matthew, come and sit down.

MATTHEW (*remaining standing*). I'm just going to give everyone a top-up.

ADAM (*reading the rules*) 'Bedlam: the ruthless card game of ever-changing rules. The object of the game is to be the first player to be out of cards by discarding cards of matching colour or value onto previously discarded cards until / all your cards are gone' –

EDITH. No, wait, wait –

SHEENA (*drinking, interrupting* ADAM). Hang on, hang on –

ADAM. What?

EDITH. Read more slowly. We need to know how to do this.

ADAM. Fine, someone else do it.

MATTHEW. Guys, how about I just tell you as I've played before. It's really simple.

EDITH. Yes, all right then, tell us.

MATTHEW. Everyone gets dealt three cards, on the cards are numbers of different colours. The aim of the game is very simply to get rid of all your cards. But you can only put down a card if it has the same number or colour as the previous card.

EDITH. What does that mean?

MATTHEW. Well, if I put down a red five, then the next player can only put down another red card, of any number, or another five, of any colour. That's it. You just play the same colour or the same number. And if you can't go, you pick up.

EDITH (*happily*). Well that does sound simple. No wonder it's for children. Deal out the cards, Adam, we haven't got all day.

ADAM *deals three number cards to each person*.

MATTHEW. Yes, well, here's where it gets a bit more complicated.

EDITH. Oh… How much more complicated?

EDITH *begins to make small cleaning adjustments to the table*.

MATTHEW. We each get given a card which has a secret rule written on it. We have to obey that rule and enforce that rule on everyone else. So, for example, you might have to say a special phrase whenever you play a blue card. Or, or you might have to wave your hand in the air when it's your turn, that sort of thing. / Something silly.

ADAM *deals poorly*.

SHEENA (*drinking, interrupting*). No, no, you've done it wrong. That's terrible dealing.

MATTHEW. You've given us four.

SHEENA. My dad would make us start again.

MATTHEW. I only need three cards.

ADAM (*throwing down the cards. To* MATTHEW). You do it then.

MATTHEW *deals the remaining number cards, and gives each player a rule card.*

MATTHEW. Guys, guys, the idea is to watch everyone else and try and guess what rules they're playing by, and follow them too. Because if you catch somebody *not* following your rule you have to give them a penalty card from the deck. And if that wasn't enough –

EDITH (*cleaning*). There's more?

MATTHEW. As well as our individual rules there's also a common rule shared by everyone. (*Turning over and reading the top rule card.*) 'Players cannot say the word "card"'. If you catch someone saying the word "card" you have to enforce the rule by saying "forbidden word" and award a penalty card from the deck.'

EDITH (*cleaning*). What, what does that mean?

MATTHEW. Maybe we should do a practice round with open cards? / I think that's probably the best –

ADAM. Forbidden word.

SHEENA (*drinking, interrupting* MATTHEW). No we don't need to do a practice round – this game is for six-year-olds, how hard can it be?

EDITH. I have a different rule on my card.

ADAM. Forbidden word.

MATTHEW. We haven't started yet – we only start when the chairman announces, 'Let the Bedlam Begin.'

CARRIE. Let the Bedlam Begin! (*Shrinking, whispering for* MATTHEW*'s benefit.*) Sorry…

EDITH. You're not the chairman. Matthew, you should be the chairman: it's your game.

MATTHEW. Mum, everybody has a different rule.

EDITH. How do I know what other people's rules are?

MATTTHEW. You don't.

SHEENA. It's an observation game.

MATTHEW. You have to watch them and guess what their rule is.

CARRIE. The thing I know about myself is that I learn by doing, so can we just do it, because I'm not holding any of this in my brain.

SHEENA. I agree, I think we should just do it.

ADAM. We're waiting on you, Matt.

CARRIE. He hasn't begun the Bedlam yet.

SHEENA. He hasn't begun the Bedlam.

CARRIE. I'm so up for this! (*For* MATTHEW*'s benefit.*) In a calm way.

ADAM (*affecting an accent*). Come on then, Mao, you're holding us up.

SHEENA. Did you just call him Mao?

ADAM. He's the chairman.

EDITH. Let's start.

   CARRIE *drum rolls on the table, then stops –*

CARRIE. Sorry. Dialling it back.

MATTHEW. Let the Bedlam Begin!

For the purposes of the card game 'Bedlam', the characters hold the following rule cards. These rules do not need to be displayed to the audience.

Matthew: 'Players must announce they are taking a drink before doing so. To enforce the rule say: "liquid infraction".'

Edith: 'Players may not ask questions. To enforce the rule say: "curiosity penalty".'

Carrie: 'A player must compliment another player before drawing a card. To enforce the rule say: "failure to brown nose".'

Sheena: 'Players must sing "Five Gold Rings" before playing a five. To enforce the rule say: "lack of expression".'

Adam: 'Players must only talk in the third person. To enforce say: "(my name) says you're not speaking in the third person".'

Common rule: Players cannot say the word "card". To enforce the rule say: "forbidden word".'

(*Playing a red six.*) To start, Dad and I are going to play... this: a red six.

CARRIE. A six. Interesting.

SHEENA. Why's that interesting?

MATTHEW. It's not. Mum, it's your turn.

EDITH *helps herself to another chewable pain-relief tablet, or lozenge.*

EDITH (*cleaning, trying to remain calm*). These cards are awfully sticky –

MATTHEW. Mum, it's your turn, can you play?

EDITH (*cleaning*). Are yours the same – some sort of sticky drink?

MATTHEW. Mum, do you have either a red card or a six?

SHEENA. Did you just say that word?

MATTHEW. What word?

SHEENA. The C–A–R–D word.

MATTHEW. Oh, yeah...

SHEENA. Take a card.

MATTHEW *picks up a penalty card from the deck.*

CARRIE. You too: forbidden word! (*Decreasing in volume.*) Sorry, sorry.

SHEENA. Ah… yes, well, fair enough.

SHEENA picks up a penalty card from the deck.

EDITH. So we're not allowed to say… I understand, okay.

CARRIE (*to* SHEENA). Oh, hang on… (*Reading her card.*) Failure to brown nose.

CARRIE gives SHEENA another penalty card from the deck.

EDITH. What? What does that mean?

SHEENA. We're not allowed to say.

ADAM (*without awarding penalty cards*). Adam says you're not speaking in the third person.

SHEENA. What?

EDITH. I'm completely lost.

MATTHEW. No you're not, Mum, you're fine. Do you have a red or a six?

EDITH. I have a blue six.

SHEENA/CARRIE/ADAM. Then play it.

EDITH lays a blue six.

MATTHEW. Put it on the top here, Mum. Carrie?

CARRIE. I can't go. So I have to pick up, right?

MATTHEW/SHEENA/ADAM. Right.

CARRIE (*meeting the terms of her rule card*). Matthew, you're amazing and I love you.

CARRIE picks up a card from the deck.

EDITH. Was that a rule?

CARRIE. I'm not allowed to say.

EDITH. She said that to Matthew and then she picked up.

CARRIE. Sheena, it's your turn.

SHEENA. I can't go.

CARRIE. Then you have to pick up.

EDITH. Does she have to say that to Matthew as well?

SHEENA (*picking up a card a card from the deck*). Matthew... you're amazing and I love you.

MATTHEW *bursts into a fit of nervous laughter.*

EDITH. Is that the rule, then? We all have to tell Matthew we love him? What an odd thing to do.

CARRIE. No, the rule is: you must compliment / another player before drawing a card.

ADAM. Adam says you're not speaking in the third person: all of you pick up.

Nobody picks up despite ADAM'*s instruction.*

CARRIE. What?

EDITH. What? Do we have to speak in the third person?

MATTHEW. Matthew thinks that, yes, we have to speak in the third person.

MATTHEW *picks up two cards, giving one to* EDITH, *and one to himself and* FRANCIS.

SHEENA (*to* ADAM). Did you just make that up?

ADAM (*awarding* SHEENA *a penalty card from the deck*). Adam says you're not / speaking in the third person.

SHEENA (*drinking, interrupting*). No, that doesn't sound like a rule, are you making it up?

MATTHEW. Sheena, was that was a *liquid infraction*?

EDITH. Oh what? What does that mean?

MATTHEW. I think we should have an open round.

EDITH. Yes, please, let's have an open round.

MATTHEW. All right everybody show their cards. Everyone say what their rule is.

They all lay their cards on the table.

SHEENA (*to* ADAM). What's your actual rule, then?
  (*Reading.*) 'Players must only talk in the third person.'
  Well… you should've been enforcing that from the very
  beginning. You can't pick and choose when the rule applies.
  If you're going to play, you have to play properly.

SHEENA *returns the rule card to* ADAM.

MATTHEW. Mum, what's your rule?

EDITH. My rule is… 'Players may not ask questions.'

MATTHEW (*reading her card*). It says here: 'to enforce the
  rule say "Curiosity Penalty" and award them a penalty card.'

EDITH. If I can't ask questions how am I supposed to find out
  what the rules are?

MATTHEW. You have to pay attention. Carrie, what's yours?

CARRIE. 'A player must compliment another player before
  drawing another card.' What's yours?

MATTHEW (*reading his card*). 'Players must announce they
  are taking a drink before doing so. To enforce the rule say
  "liquid infraction".' Sheena?

SHEENA (*reading*). 'Players must sing "Five Gold Rings"
  before playing a five.'

EDITH. 'Five Gold Rings'?

MATTHEW. From 'The Twelve Days of Christmas'.

CARRIE. Only takes *one* gold ring – am I right, Sheena?

SHEENA. What?

CARRIE *flashes her ring finger.*

What are you doing – ?

MATTHEW. Are we ready to start again?

EDITH *helps herself to another chewable pain-relief tablet
or lozenge.*

EDITH (*cleaning*). Why can't we just put down cards, why do
  we have to have all these arbitrary rules?

MATTHEW. Mum, all games have arbitrary rules. That's literally what a game is. Get the ball in the hole, but don't let it off the field. Go down the snakes and up ladders.

EDITH. Then what's the point?

MATTHEW. The point is to have fun, Mum.

ADAM (*affecting an accent*). That's right, Billy the Bed-wetter. Isn't everybody having fun?

MATTHEW. Is everybody ready? Let the Bedlam Begin!

CARRIE lays a card, then SHEENA, then ADAM, then MATTHEW/FRANCIS and then EDITH. CARRIE lays another card.

EDITH. Carrie, you're being rather quiet.

SHEENA lays a card, then ADAM, then MATTHEW/ FRANCIS over the next few lines.

CARRIE. Oh, well, I don't want to overdo it and embarrass Matthew.

MATTHEW. Hey…

EDITH. Matthew embarrasses very easily. He's what I call 'exasperatingly oversensitive'.

Rule 1 becomes live; it will remain live until MATTHEW gets a compliment.

MATTHEW. *Mum?* Don't say that… (*Sitting, eating.*) It's not true.

EDITH. Just ignore him. You're an actress, if you can't entertain everybody then what good are you?

Rule 2 becomes live: it will remain live until CARRIE gets a laugh.

(*Laying a yellow five.*) Oh look, I can play: a yellow five.

CARRIE. Oh, oh… (*Standing, dancing around, singing.*) Five gold rings! Four colly birds, three French hens, two turtledoves and a partridge in a pear tree!

MATTHEW (*sitting and eating*). I'm not exasperatingly oversensitive. Am I?

Having failed to get a laugh, CARRIE *must tell another joke.*

CARRIE (*standing, dancing around*). Oh, I know a rude version! On the first day of Christmas my true love gave to me, a hand-job in a pear tree!

MATTHEW. I've no idea why you'd say that about me.

SHEENA *wordlessly gives* EDITH *a penalty card from the pack.*

EDITH. Thank you, Carrie, please sit down, it's your turn.

CARRIE. On the second day of Christmas my true love gave to me, two bulging balls and a –

MATTHEW *restrains* CARRIE *by sitting on her lap, he fakes a laugh.*

MATTHEW (*sitting, eating, forcing a laugh*). Ha ha! That's hilarious.

Having got a laugh, Rule 2 is no longer live.

CARRIE. Why thank you, baby. I'll be here all night.

EDITH. Matthew, don't speak with your mouth full.

CARRIE. *You're* hilarious. And I love you.

Having got a compliment, Rule 1 is no longer live.

MATTHEW (*standing*). Thanks. Thank you. Sorry, Mum. Carrie, it's your turn.

CARRIE (*laying her penultimate card*). Oh sorry, here. Sheena?

SHEENA *is about to lay a card when* FRANCIS *tries to lay a card instead.*

MATTHEW (*remaining standing*). Actually, Dad, it's not our turn yet.

FRANCIS *insists on playing the card.*

We're going round the circle and it's Sheena's turn.

EDITH (*cleaning*). Why don't we skip Sheena's turn. / I go after Francis.

SHEENA (*drinking, interrupting*). No, hang on, I'm not missing a turn, that's not fair.

FRANCIS *tries to speak – he wants to insist that he hasn't made a mistake, the only word he can say is 'No'.*

EDITH. I know it's confusing, isn't it? I've no idea what's going on.

FRANCIS *repeats the word 'No'.*

No, I'm sorry, I didn't mean *you're* confused, I mean *it's* confusing.

ADAM (*attempting to calm* FRANCIS). Hey, hey, Dad, it's all right. Listen, Carrie, did you know you were sitting across from the 'Crime Silk of the Year' three years running?

CARRIE. I've no idea what that means, but it sounds good.

ADAM. It's the best. Dad was the very best.

FRANCIS *brightens.*

This is the man that UK Chambers called – (*Affecting accent.*) The Phenomenon.

CARRIE. Very impressive.

ADAM. Our grandfather was a solicitor, but that wasn't good enough for Dad. He was determined to be a barrister, and not only that, a judge.

FRANCIS *gestures to his sons with his good hand.*

EDITH (*translating*). Yes, our boys will make fantastic solicitors one day.

FRANCIS *repeats the word 'No'.*

No, no that's right… barristers. Not solicitors, barristers.

ADAM (*affecting an accent*). Judge Dredd over here thinks solicitors are *second class*.

CARRIE. But you're both soli–

MATTHEW *shushes* CARRIE.

EDITH. Whose turn is it please? We skipped Sheena, Francis played, so… it's my turn.

EDITH *lays a card, followed by* CARRIE.

CARRIE (*playing her final card*). Oh, oh, that's my last card, I win! / Do I win?

SHEENA (*drinking, interrupting*). No, no! Third person! Third person! Pick up a card, Carrie!

CARRIE. Oh what, no…!

CARRIE *picks up a penalty card from the deck.*

ADAM (*affecting an accent*). I've figured out something about this game, chaps: I think it might be impossible to win.

MATTHEW. That's loser talk if ever I heard it.

SHEENA. Exactly. Exactly. Thank you. Loser!

ADAM (*awarding* SHEENA *a penalty card from the deck*). Adam says you're not speaking in the third person.

CARRIE. Carrie's wondering, is that a six or a nine?

EDITH. Carrie asked a question: curiosity penalty.

ADAM (*awarding* EDITH *a penalty card from his own hand*). Adam says you're not talking in the third person.

SHEENA (*drinking, interrupting*). No, no, did you just try and palm one off from your own hand?

ADAM (*serving* SHEENA *another penalty card from his own hand*). Liquid infraction.

SHEENA (*returning the card to* ADAM). That's cheating; take it back.

ADAM. Why's that cheating?

SHEENA (*serving him a penalty card from the deck*). Curiosity penalty.

ADAM. Why's that cheating?

SHEENA (*serving him another penalty card from the deck*). Curiosity penalty.

ADAM. What's a curiosity penalty?

SHEENA. You know perfectly well.

MATTHEW. Adam. Play the game.

ADAM. Should I do that, Matty? Should I play the game
properly? (*With venom.*) Perhaps I should phone a friend?

MATTHEW. Come on –

ADAM. Perhaps I should phone an extra-special friend, for a
good long chat, what do you think?

CARRIE (*serving him a penalty card from the deck*). Curiosity
penalty!

ADAM (*serving himself a penalty card for every question,
affecting an accent*). Another one, Barbie? Really? What
about this? How about that?

SHEENA (*drinking, interrupting*). No, no stop it, stop it –

ADAM (*continuing to serve himself penalty cards, amassing a
stack*). Why should I stop it, Clogs? Am I doing it wrong?

CARRIE. Third person, third person!

ADAM (*awarding himself yet more penalty cards*). Am I not
speaking in the third person, Barbie?

CARRIE. Barbie thinks you are not, / have another card.

SHEENA (*drinking, interrupting*). No, shut up, Carrie.

Rule 2 becomes live; it will remain live until CARRIE *gets a
laugh.*

ADAM (*affecting an accent, continuing to award himself
penalty cards*). Am I losing, Barbie?

CARRIE (*standing, dancing around, awarding* ADAM *a
penalty card*). Barbie thinks Adam is definitely losing!

ADAM (*affecting an accent, taking the card*). Am I really,
Barbie? Is this not how you play the game?

CARRIE (*standing, dancing around*). Barbie feels that there is a
discussion to be had at some point about what the fuck is
going on!

CARRIE *and* ADAM *laugh.*

Having received a laugh, Rule 2 is no longer live.

(*Sitting.*) Thank you very much, I'll be here all night!

Scene Four

The following rules are displayed to the audience for the duration of the scene:

Rule 1: Matthew must sit and eat to tell a lie… until he gets a compliment

Rule 2: Carrie must stand and dance around to tell a joke… until she gets a laugh

Rule 3: Sheena must drink and interrupt to contradict… **until she has the last word**

Rule 4. Adam must affect an accent and name-call to mock

Rule 5. Edith must clean and self-medicate to keep calm

From now on, once SHEENA *has started contradicting, she cannot stop contradicting until she has the last word.*

SHEENA. We think Adam's trying to undermine the game. We think he's not taking this seriously. Just like he doesn't take anything seriously.

ADAM (*serving a penalty card*). Adam says that Sheena's speaking in the first person plural not the third person singular. Sheena needs to figure that out.

Rule 3 becomes live: SHEENA *must have the last word or make another contradiction.*

While Sheena finds a copy of *Grammar for Dummies* / Adam is going to –

SHEENA (*drinking, interrupting*). No, no, actually, I was speaking in the third person.

ADAM (*awarding her a penalty card*). First person singular – getting closer.

CARRIE. Sheena, that was a / liquid infraction.

Having failed to get the last word, SHEENA *must make another contradiction.*

SHEENA (*drinking, interrupting, returning her penalty cards to the pile*). No, no I'm not accepting those penalty cards –

CARRIE (*awarding a penalty card*). Liquid infraction –

ADAM (*awarding a penalty card*). Still first person singular.

SHEENA. – because you're not playing properly, you are deliberately sabotaging yourself like you always do. Why don't you just try like everybody else? You don't need to win – nobody's asking you to be a winner – you just need to give it a go. But you can't do that, can you? Because your mum's right: why are you so terrified of losing?

ADAM. Curiosity penalty.

SHEENA. It's because you take it as evidence –

ADAM. Curiosity penalty, take the card.

SHEENA shoves a mince pie into ADAM*'s mouth essentially gagging him.*

SHEENA. I'm speaking! You lost your nerve bowling in front of twenty-eight thousand people and you've never found it again. And that's why you're terrified of losing, because you take it as evidence of what you deep down believe about yourself, which is that you're already a loser!

ADAM *is unable to respond.*

Thank you. End of argument.

Having got the last word, Rule 3 is no longer live.

Scene Five

The following rules are displayed to the audience for the duration of the scene:

Rule 1: Matthew must sit and eat to tell a lie… until he gets a compliment

Rule 2: Carrie must stand and dance around to tell a joke… until she gets a laugh

Rule 3: Sheena must drink and interrupt to contradict… until she has the last word

Rule 4. Adam must affect an accent and name-call to mock… **until he has deflected blame**

Rule 5. Edith must clean and self-medicate to keep calm

From now on, once ADAM *has started mocking, he cannot stop mocking until he has deflected blame.*

MATTHEW. Look, this 'third person rule' is a bit tricky, why don't just we change it?

EDITH. That's a good idea.

MATTHEW. Adam, why don't you have a new rule? (*Taking the top rule card off the deck and reading.*) 'Players must announce "Have a nice day!" after awarding a penalty card.

EDITH. Oh that's nice.

CARRIE. Yes, that's friendly, I like that.

MATTHEW. How about that, Adam? To enforce the rule you have to say 'Lack of good wishes'.

ADAM *stands and makes to exit to the garden for a cigarette.*

EDITH. Where are you going?

MATTHEW. Or, or… (*Reading another rule card.*) 'Players must say "All for one and one for all!" before playing a number one.'

SHEENA. Adam, I'm sorry, I didn't mean for it to come out like that. It's just so frustrating watching you do this to yourself. You're your own worst enemy.

Rule 4 becomes live; ADAM *must mock until he has successfully deflected blame.*

ADAM (*affecting an accent, holding an imaginary phone receiver to his ear*). Hello, is that kettle?... No, don't worry, I'll leave a message. Tell him it's pot calling. Tell him I said he's black.

EDITH. Adam, darling, there's no need to be sarcastic.

Having failed to deflect blame onto SHEENA, ADAM *must continue to mock.*

ADAM (*affecting an accent*). That wasn't sarcasm, that was self-defence: the Bean Queen over there can't seem to stop attacking me.

Rule 3 becomes live: SHEENA *must contradict until she has the last word.*

EDITH. She's not attacking you, darling, nobody's attacking you. Why don't you just carry on with the game?

Having once again failed to deflect blame onto SHEENA, ADAM *must continue to mock.*

ADAM (*affecting an accent*). Yes she is. Pretty Polly doesn't care who she hurts as long as she's right... (*Imitating a parrot.*) I'm right, / I'm right, I'm right.

SHEENA (*drinking, interrupting*). No, that's not true, that's not fair.

Having still failed to deflect blame onto SHEENA, ADAM *must continue to mock.*

ADAM (*affecting an accent*). Knowing your parents – *Fred and Rose* – I think you felt growing up that you had to have an opinion or they wouldn't approve of you.

Having failed to get the last word, SHEENA *must make another contradiction.*

SHEENA. What? That's simply... [not true]

SHEENA *attempts to drink, but* ADAM *confiscates her glass. Unable to drink,* SHEENA *is unable to contradict. She goes in search of more alcohol.*

EDITH. Now come on, darlings, get on with the game. Who is going next?

ADAM (*affecting an accent*). The only way to be heard in your *University Challenge* house was to be louder and more obnoxious than everybody else.

CARRIE. I think it's Sheena's turn.

EDITH. Sheena, darling –

SHEENA *reaches for the cognac.*

– darling, the Christmas cognac is for *after* lunch.

ADAM (*confiscating the cognac, affecting an accent*). You always have to have the answer, Anne Robinson, otherwise you're afraid people will think you're stupid. / Because that's what *you* think about *yourself.*

SHEENA (*stealing* FRANCIS*'s glass, drinking, interrupting*). I am not stupid!

ADAM (*affecting an accent*). I didn't say you *were* stupid, Clogs, I said you *think* you're stupid.

MATTHEW. Hey, guys, guys, why don't we say this whole thing was my fault. I should've known better than to bring a game no one had played before. Let's say I'm to blame.

ADAM (*without an accent*). See, there you go, it's Matthew's fault.

Having deflected blame onto MATTHEW*, Rule 4 is no longer live.*

Thank you, Matthew. / Apology accepted.

Still having failed to get the last word, SHEENA *must continue to contradict.*

SHEENA (*drinking, interrupting*). No, Matthew, it's not your fault, it's a brilliant game, and if it wasn't for Adam we'd all be having a *really good time.*

Rule 4 once again becomes live: ADAM *must mock until he has deflected blame.*

ADAM (*affecting an accent*). D'you want to say that again, Brian Blessed, I don't think they heard you in France?

EDITH (*holding up a rule card*). Why don't we try this new rule: 'All for one and one for all'? / I think that's really Christmas.

SHEENA (*drinking, interrupting, snatching the card from* EDITH). No, I've got a new rule for Adam... (*Finding a pen and writing on the card.*) Adam must announce 'I'm a scaredy-cat' before being sarcastic. To enforce the rule say, 'Get over yourself'.

ADAM (*affecting an accent*). You're just scribbling illegibly, Jackson Pollack, / I can't read any of that.

SHEENA (*drinking, interrupting, serving him with a penalty card*). Get over yourself!

ADAM. Fine, if we're changing the rules... (*Taking the pen and writing on a card, affecting an accent.*) Grumpy, the smallest dwarf, must announce 'I'm also a scaredy-cat' before talking over other people. To enforce the rule say, 'Pipe down, you insufferable bore.'

SHEENA (*drinking, interrupting*). No, no, actually, this isn't funny, this is serious –

ADAM (*serving her a penalty card, affecting an accent*). Pipe down, you insufferable bore!

MATTHEW. Adam, slow down, there's no need to be mean.

ADAM (*to* MATTHEW, *affecting an accent*). D'you want me to write a card for you, Matty? Sorry, I meant *Fatty, the twatty.* You want everybody to know what your card would say? / *Twatty* must announce...

MATTHEW. No, no, Adam, don't write that –

EDITH. All right, all right, enough. I think we should try a different game. / What about Charades?

Rules 3 and 4 remain live: SHEENA *must continue to contradict;* ADAM *must continue to mock.*

SHEENA (*drinking, interrupting*). No, Edith, there's no point, there's no point in trying again. I really don't think Adam and I can play together any more. In fact, unless he's prepared to change we might as well call the whole thing off. Right now.

EDITH. Well that's a bit drastic. / I think Charades is a bit less –

SHEENA (*drinking, interrupting*). No, all right, actually, actually I'm going to give you *one last chance*. One more game but you have to really try, you have to *really* make an effort to do your best. Put yourself out there – see what happens. I mean it, I'm not bluffing: *this is all or nothing.*

ADAM (*affecting an accent*) The ultimate decision-maker from Jeremy Paxman!

SHEENA (*drinking, interrupting*). No, not in that ridiculous voice. If you're going to change you have to drop the silly voices and speak properly. So, what do you say? Are you in or out?

Pause.

Adam, in or out?

Rule 4 is still live: ADAM *must continue to mock until he has deflected blame.*

ADAM (*affecting an accent*). Is there an option to 'shake it all about', little 'un?

EDITH. Adam, darling, don't be silly.

SHEENA (*drinking, interrupting*). No, that's it, Adam's made his decision. This is his doing.

ADAM (*affecting an accent*). How is this my fault, George Best? Let's see you put down the glass of wine / and then we'll talk about *trying again*.

SHEENA (*drinking, interrupting*). No, all right, fine, I'm not blaming you, I'm not blaming you, I'm not blaming you.

Having deflected blame from himself, Rule 4 is no longer live.

ADAM. Good. / Thank you.

SHEENA (*drinking, interrupting*). No, no, thank you. Finally we know where we stand. Sometimes you have to accept when you're beaten.

ADAM *doesn't respond.*

So that's it, then. Game over.

Having got the last word, Rule 3 is no longer live.

End of argument.

The kitchen timer rings out.

EDITH. Perfect timing: lunch is ready! Could I have some help serving up please? Hello?

ADAM *and* SHEENA *look at one another, digesting the realisation that they have essentially just agreed to divorce.*

MATTHEW. Carrie, could you help Mum, or are you going sit there doing nothing like a stale muffin?

Rule 2 becomes live: it will remain live until CARRIE *gets a laugh.*

CARRIE (*standing, dancing around*). I'm so hungry I could eat the back leg of the Lamb of God!

Nobody laughs. Rule 2 remains live; CARRIE *must tell another joke.*

(*Standing, dancing around.*) Edith, this smells amazing. If this is an audition for my future mother-in-law, as a heads-up, I can certainly see what you bring to the table!

EDITH. Oh Carrie, you're such a card.

CARRIE (*standing, dancing around*). Forbidden word, hah!

EDITH *forces a laugh. Rule 2 is no longer live.*

(*Sitting at the table.*) Thanks very much, I'll be here all night.

EDITH. Is anyone else going to come and help, or are you stuck in time over there?

SHEENA. We were. But not any more.

SHEENA goes to help EDITH. MATTHEW tries to offer ADAM sympathy; ADAM shrugs him off.

EDITH. Sit wherever you like, my darlings. Not there, Carrie, I want Adam to sit there next to Dad.

FRANCIS tries to speak, he wants to sit next to CARRIE – he is able to say the word 'girl'.

You want to sit next to Carrie? Well, aren't you flavour of the month?

CARRIE sits beside FRANCIS. He reaches for her hair.

EDITH. I'll sit on the other side, then. Adam why don't you sit next to me, and Matthew why don't go next to Carrie. And, Sheena, you can come between the two boys. (*To* FRANCIS.) Maybe she doesn't want to let her hair down, Francis.

CARRIE (*unhooking his hands from her hair*). All right, all right. (*Letting her hair down.*) There.

FRANCIS reaches again for her hair. ADAM stops his hand.

ADAM. All right, leave her alone. She's not a doll.

EDITH. Adam, sit down please. Now we don't stand on ceremony in this family, help yourselves.

MATTHEW. Who's going to carve?

EDITH. Oh yes. Seeing as he's not quite able to this year –

FRANCIS insists on carving the turkey.

Yes, I know, but it might be a bit tricky, why don't we ask one of the –

MATTHEW (*remaining standing*). I'll do it.

ADAM. I'll do it, I'm the oldest.

FRANCIS demands to carve the turkey.

EDITH. Why doesn't Adam do it seeing as he's the man of his house?

Rule 3 becomes live: SHEENA *must contradict until she has the last word.*

SHEENA (*drinking, interrupting*). Actually, I'll do it.

FRANCIS *attempts to carve the turkey.*

EDITH (*attempting to help* FRANCIS). All right, wait a moment. Why don't I just…?

FRANCIS *swipes at* EDITH.

MATTHEW. Mum – !

EDITH (*backing off*). No, no, right you are, you know best.

FRANCIS *attempts to carve the turkey. He is unable to fully grip the knife. He is unable to pierce the turkey breast with the fork. The family watch, unsure what to do.*

ADAM. Dad, why don't I – ?

FRANCIS *turns the knife in his direction.* ADAM *backs down.*

The knife slips dangerously. They all draw breath. Eventually SHEENA *interrupts.*

SHEENA (*drinking, interrupting*). No, I'm sorry, but this is actually dangerous –

EDITH. Sheena, don't –

SHEENA. – we can't just watch while Carrie loses an eye. I'll take the knife.

FRANCIS *doesn't resist, he surrenders the carving knife to* SHEENA, *dejected.*

EDITH. Traditionally it should be one of the boys. / Francis taught them both to –

SHEENA (*drinking, interrupting*). Sometimes tradition is wrong. I don't see why the 'man of the house' should be the one to carve… (*Haphazardly hacking into the turkey.*) I mean, whenever did he actually cook the damn thing in the first place?

MATTHEW. Sheena, be careful…

SHEENA. A woman slaves for hours over a hot stove just so a man can lord it over his family in a, a flagrant peacock display of, of knife-wielding? No thank you, I don't think so.

EDITH. You don't need to kill it, you just need to carve it.

SHEENA. Cos single mothers do very well, actually. Men make you think you can't wire a plug but you can. You can. You can find the television programme you recorded. You can change a halogen bulb. Just you watch me put up a *fucking tree house*.

EDITH. Sheena –

By this point, SHEENA *has made an utter mess of the turkey – half-cut flesh flayed in all directions. She finishes with a flourish, stabbing the knife into the turkey breast.*

SHEENA. Carved! End of.

Nobody responds.

Having got the last word, Rule 3 is no longer live.

EDITH. So… Everybody… help yourselves. Francis, what can I get you, a bit of everything?

FRANCIS *pushes his plate away.*

(*Offering him a spoon.*) Darling, you need to eat something – why don't you just try a little – ?

FRANCIS *rejects the spoon, food spills over* EDITH.

Is everybody helping themselves to gravy? Adam, have more potatoes than that.

EDITH *stands up from the table and goes in search of pain medication. But her packet of sachets is empty and her pain-relief lozenges are missing. She searches the room.*

ADAM. This isn't for me, it's for Emma, I'm taking her up some lunch.

SHEENA. Adam, we agreed, she's having less carbohydrates than that.

ADAM. Fewer, fewer, fewer carbohydrates. And you agreed that with no one but yourself.

Rule 3 becomes live once again: SHEENA *must contradict until she has the last word.*

Tell you what, I'll take *my daughter* her Christmas lunch and you can take her three sprouts and a chestnut, and we'll see which of us she prefers.

SHEENA (*drinking, interrupting*). No, we're not having this argument. *My daughter* is sticking to her diet.

EDITH. Matthew, have you moved my lozenges?

MATTHEW. Adam, Sheena's researched this, she knows her stuff. And if it works, and you don't give it a try then you've only got yourself to blame.

Rule 4 becomes live once again: ADAM *must mock until he has deflected blame.*

ADAM (*affecting an accent*). Oh thanks, Pamela Stephenson, your counselling services are really appreciated. / You should think about a career change –

SHEENA (*drinking, interrupting*). Actually, they are appreciated… (*Taking* MATTHEW'*s hand.*) Matthew is a real comfort.

CARRIE. Isn't he? (*Taking* MATTHEW'*s other hand.*) I'm so lucky to have him. In fact, we have an announcement to make. We have some big news, don't we, baby?

Rule 1 becomes live; it will remain live until MATTHEW *gets a compliment.*

MATTHEW *tries to sit and eat, but* CARRIE *and* SHEENA *are still tightly holding his hands making it impossible. Unable to sit and eat he is unable to lie.*

MATTHEW. We can tell them later.

CARRIE. Let's tell them now.

ADAM (*affecting an accent*). Yeah, tell us, Mr Kipling, / what's the big announcement?

SHEENA (*drinking, interrupting*). He doesn't have to tell us anything if he doesn't want to.

EDITH (*searching, without calm*). Matthew, what have you done with my lozenges?

MATTHEW *struggles to sit and eat.*

ADAM (*affecting an accent*). I'm just trying to support Barbie. / Don't blame me.

SHEENA (*drinking, interrupting*). No, you're just trying to deflect attention from yourself.

CARRIE. Well if you won't tell them, I will.

MATTHEW *is forced to lower his face to his plate to eat.*

Everybody, Matthew and I are getting –

MATTHEW (*sitting, eating*). A dog. We're getting a dog!

CARRIE. What?

ADAM (*affecting an accent*). Wow, that is important and significant news, Cookie Monster. / Seriously, how hungry are you?

SHEENA (*clicking her fingers in* ADAM*'S face, drinking, interrupting*). Hey, hey, stop changing the subject, I'm trying to have a conversation with you.

CARRIE (*to* MATTHEW). I'm trying to make an announcement.

MATTHEW (*sitting, eating*). I'm just telling them the good news.

ADAM (*affecting an accent*). I'm not going to stop doing anything, Clogs, until you stop interrupting me. / If you keep interrupting me then I can't –

SHEENA (*drinking*). I'm not going to stop interrupting you until you stop speaking in that ridiculous voice. You're not a cartoon!

EDITH. Matthew, they were in this drawer. They were in this drawer.

CARRIE (*to* MATTHEW). What's the matter with you? Why are you so afraid to tell them – ?

MATTHEW (*sitting, eating*). I'm not afraid to tell anyone –

ADAM (*affecting an accent*). Then we're going to go round and round forever, aren't we, Clogs?

SHEENA. Stop calling me Clogs, I hate it when you call me Clogs!

ADAM (*affecting an accent*). It's cos you're so clever, Clogs!

SHEENA throws a potato (*or similar*) *at* ADAM, *it hits* EDITH *or something dear to her.*

Beat.

SHEENA. Edith… I'm…

Having been unable to find her pain medication, EDITH *is unable to calm herself.*

EDITH (*without cleaning, without calm*). How dare you. All of you. How could you be so selfish? You're behaving like little children –

ADAM (*affecting an accent*). Don't look at me, Matron, she's the one –

EDITH (*without cleaning, without calm*). You can't even sit at the table for five minutes without scoring points off each other. / What's the matter with you?

SHEENA (*drinking, interrupting*). I'm not trying to score points, Edith, I'm –

EDITH (*without cleaning, without calm*). I've been cooking for a week so that you can have devils on horseback *as well* as pigs in blankets; and so your father can have mashed potatoes *as well* as roast potatoes, and so Emma can have coins *as well* as charms in the Christmas pudding, which she now won't even see because / she won't even come downstairs to say hello –

SHEENA (*drinking, interrupting*). Of course she'll see it, Edith, she's just not joining us for lunch –

MATTHEW (*sitting, eating*). Mum, we're not taking any of that for granted –

ADAM (*affecting an accent*). Come on, *Mummy*, don't be like that –

EDITH. I am not finished! One lunch, that's all I asked of you. One lunch to honour your father: this wonderful, generous man, who has worked tirelessly all his life to give you the best of everything: the school fees, university fees, the interviews, the *jobs*. Not to mention the deposits for your houses. And now Emma, who pays her school fees? The last time I checked it wasn't any of you. And you can't even sit through one meal for him – you should be ashamed!

As she comforts him, FRANCIS *gropes* CARRIE. *She stifles a shriek.*

What's the matter?

CARRIE. Nothing. It was… probably nothing.

In full view of everyone, FRANCIS *gropes* CARRIE *a second time. She shrieks and recoils.*

Scene Six

The following rules are displayed to the audience for the duration of the scene:

Rule 1: Matthew must sit and eat to tell a lie... until he gets a compliment

Rule 2: Carrie must stand and dance around to tell a joke... until she gets a laugh

Rule 3: Sheena must drink and interrupt to contradict... until she has the last word

Rule 4. Adam must affect an accent and name-call to mock... until he has deflected blame

Rule 5. Edith must clean and self-medicate to keep calm... **until she gets reassurance**

From now on, once EDITH *has started calming herself, she cannot stop calming herself until she gets reassurance.*

At the top of the scene, Rules 1, 3 and 4 are still live.

Rule 5 immediately becomes live; it will remain live until EDITH *gets reassurance.*

EDITH *approaches* FRANCIS *and retrieves a packet of post-operative pain medication from his shirt pocket. She swallows one tablet with a glass of wine. She begins to clean obsessively.*

CARRIE. Please don't worry, I'm sorry / I overreacted.

SHEENA (*drinking, interrupting*). No, no you don't need to apologise.

ADAM (*affecting an accent*). Damn right – it's the General who should be apologising. He's the worst of all!

Having deflected blame onto FRANCIS, *Rule 4 is no longer live.*

EDITH (*cleaning*). Now everyone calm down, I'm sure Francis didn't mean any harm. Isn't that right?

ADAM (*without an accent*). Mum, you're not glossing over this. Dad just groped Carrie.

EDITH (*cleaning*). Please, there's no need to let the food go cold, is there? Matthew?

ADAM (*to* MATTHEW). You saw that, right?

EDITH (*cleaning*). Matthew, darling?

MATTHEW (*sitting, eating*). Dad's very confused – I'm sure he didn't know what he was doing.

EDITH. Thank you, darling.

Having got reassurance from MATTHEW, *Rule 5 is no longer live.*

You're such a support.

Having got a compliment, Rule 1 is no longer live.

MATTHEW (*standing*). Thank you, Mum.

ADAM. Are you all determined to cover up for him? This is what he does! / What he's always –

SHEENA (*drinking, interrupting*). Adam, don't, don't. Now you're making a scene!

Rule 4 becomes live once again: it will remain live until ADAM *has deflected blame.*

EDITH. You know full well your father's not in his right mind.

ADAM (*affecting an accent*). What are you talking about? This *is* his mind. It's always been his mind – he just can't hide it any more – (*To* FRANCIS, *affecting an accent.*) can you, General? Come on – we're taking a trip to the naughty corner.

ADAM *stands, takes the handles of his father's wheelchair.*

EDITH *moves quickly to stop him – blocking his way.*

EDITH. Where on earth do you think you're going?

ADAM (*affecting an accent*). *Daddy's* going to the naughty corner. That's where he sent us, when we misbehaved at the table. Or interrupted him. Or disagreed with him in any way.

MATTHEW. Now come on, Adam…

EDITH. Don't be so *cruel*. Put your father back right now.

ADAM (*affecting an accent*). No cruelty here – don't you worry. I'll even let him take his food with him – which is more than he ever did for us. (*Grabs* FRANCIS*'s plate, places it on* FRANCIS*'s lap*.) Some breast meat for you there, General? / You like that, don't you?

SHEENA. No, Adam. Stop it.

CARRIE. Please, don't do this on my account –

EDITH. Yes, don't do this on her account. It's hardly your father's fault when she… puts them on display like that.

Rule 2 becomes live; it will remain live until CARRIE *scores a point.*

CARRIE (*standing, dancing around*). Well I *was* going to come wearing a pair of curtains – but then I didn't want to wear the same thing as you, Edith…

Despite herself, SHEENA *laughs. Rule 2 is no longer live.* CARRIE *sits.*

ADAM (*to* FRANCIS, *affecting an accent*). Well, looks like your luck's in, Your Honour. I thought Mum only put up with your antics when you kept them out of sight, but she seems fine with them out in the open, too!

Rule 5 becomes live again; it will remain live until EDITH *gets reassurance.*

EDITH. This is too much – it's too much. Where are my – ?

EDITH reaches for the painkillers in FRANCIS*'s shirt pocket. ADAM snatches them from her.*

MATTHEW. Guys, guys, everybody sit down –

ADAM (*affecting an accent*). These are Dad's painkillers, Mummy dearest – serious opiates, you can't pop them like they're Tic Tacs.

MATTHEW. Guys, the gravy's getting a skin on it.

Unable to self-medicate, EDITH *is unable to keep calm.*

EDITH (*without calm*). You have *always* been jealous of your father! We're all afraid to say it, but it's true. It's not Francis's fault he was a brilliant lawyer, and you're just a… just a…

ADAM (*affecting an accent*). You think I envy Skeletor's legal career? I wanted to play cricket!

EDITH. Well it's *certainly* not your father's fault that you couldn't play cricket.

ADAM (*affecting an accent*). I *could* play cricket, Mum, I *was* playing cricket – *beautiful* cricket! But that wasn't good enough for Darth Vader. 'Line and length, son, line and length.' I tried to be Glen McGrath for you and I ended up *nobody*!

EDITH *goes in search of other medication.*

EDITH. He was trying to help you; he only ever had your best interests at heart.

ADAM (*affecting an accent*). When was Dad interested in anyone but himself? It's always been about him – he manipulated all of us into being whoever *he* wanted us to be. He knew Judy wanted to be an actor, but he wouldn't let him –

MATTHEW. Come on, Adam, Dad got me my first singing teacher –

ADAM (*affecting an accent*). Yeah, and then he *shagged* your singing teacher six ways to Sunday – (*To* FRANCIS.) didn't you, Don Juan? Even now, from his bloody wheelchair, he's still manipulating the whole bloody lot of us…!

MATTHEW. All right, that's enough. You need to go for a walk.

EDITH (*taking a pill*). Yes, out. Get him out – he's ruining everything.

MATTHEW *puts an arm on* ADAM.

ADAM (*affecting an accent*). You don't want to touch me, Shirley.

MATTHEW. You need to take a time-out, okay, you're upsetting everybody.

ADAM (*affecting an accent*). You're going to swoop in and play the hero, are you? Matthew the Peacekeeper.

MATTHEW. Someone needs to keep the peace, and it's obviously not going to be you.

ADAM (*affecting an accent*). Well if you're such a peacekeeper – why are you trying to fuck my wife?

Beat.

Rule 1 becomes live: it will remain live until MATTHEW *gets a compliment.*

Rule 2 becomes live: it will remain live until CARRIE *gets a laugh.*

All five rules are now live.

CARRIE (*standing, dancing around*). Oh my God… that had *better* / be a joke…

SHEENA (*interrupting, drinking, stunned*). No, no, no, not good!

For the first time, all five rules are live at the same time.

EDITH *pops more pills.*

MATTHEW *sinks into a chair, grabs a turkey leg.*

MATTHEW. Why would you say something like that? That's… (*Sitting, eating.*) that's preposterous.

ADAM (*affecting an accent*). Did Fatty not tell you – he phones my wife every day, for hours at a time, when he knows / I'm out of the house?

SHEENA (*drinking, interrupting* ADAM). Adam, Adam, don't –

CARRIE (*standing, dancing around*). That… doesn't sound like Matthew… He's not a phone person. He doesn't even like phone *sex*, let alone phone *chats*…

ADAM (*affecting an accent*). I can show you the phone bill, Barbie. / Two hours, three hours at a time.

SHEENA (*drinking, interrupting*). It's not how it sounds – Matthew just gives me advice –

ADAM (*affecting an accent*). Oh, I'm sure that's what he wants you to think. Matthew the shoulder to cry on. Matthew the port in a storm. (*To* MATTHEW.) Enough with the foreplay, mate – why don't you tell her the truth?

MATTHEW (*sitting, eating, to* CARRIE). I honestly don't know what he's talking about.

ADAM (*confiscating* MATTHEW'*s food, affecting an accent*). Put the turkey leg down, Barney Rubble, and step away from the table.

ADAM *pulls* MATTHEW *up out of the chair.*

MATTHEW *breaks free and sits in a different chair.*

MATTHEW (*sitting, eating*). I don't know why you're saying all this – it's so unfair.

ADAM (*confiscating* MATTHEW'*s food, affecting an accent*). I said stop stuffing your face, / you little liar, and get up.

Again ADAM *pulls* MATTHEW *up out of the chair.*

SHEENA (*drinking, interrupting*). No, Adam, stop it, stop it!

MATTHEW *grabs a handful of food and again pulls out of* ADAM'*s grip.* ADAM *chases him.* MATTHEW *sits in a third chair.*

MATTHEW (*sitting, eating*). I'm not lying. I promise, I'm not lying.

ADAM *tips him out of the chair onto the floor.*

ADAM (*affecting an accent*). You want her, you little covetous shit! Admit it.

MATTHEW (*sitting on the floor, eating*). I swear I'm not a liar.

ADAM *lifts him from under his armpits.*

ADAM (*affecting an accent*). For once in your fat life, Fat Boy, stand up and tell the truth!

Unable to sit and eat MATTHEW *is unable to tell a lie.*

MATTHEW. I don't '*want*' her…

SHEENA (*drinking, interrupting*). Thank you…

MATTHEW. I love her! I'm in love with her! From the first day she walked onto our front lawn, until this second, right now, I've been completely crazy about her. My whole life… (*To* SHEENA.) you've just been this perfect angel making everything else bearable. No matter how fucking awful things got at home, no matter how shit my life gets, when it's just darkness, and misery and nothing, you're the one thing, the *only* thing, that keeps me going. I loved you before he did, I love you now he's stopped, I just love you, Sheena, I love you!

Long pause.

ADAM (*affecting an accent*). I knew it. I knew it! Thank you!

Having deflected blame onto MATTHEW, *Rule 4 is no longer live.*

CARRIE (*standing, jigging around*). Are you fucking kidding me?

ADAM. See? Didn't I tell you? / Did I not tell you?

SHEENA (*drinking, interrupting*). No, no he doesn't. He doesn't love me. Not like that.

CARRIE (*standing, jigging around*). You just proposed to me! Now *that's* a fucking joke…

ADAM. Oh my God – you proposed? / This calls for champagne!

SHEENA (*drinking, interrupting*). Adam, don't, stop it – you're making it worse!

Rule 4 becomes live once again; it will remain live until ADAM *has deflected blame.*

ADAM (*affecting an accent, grabbing a bottle of champagne from the table*). Offers out to both recruits on the same day? Well it's hardly surprising: Fatty always did want to have his cake *and* eat it. (*Raising the champagne bottle.*) Mazel Tov! (*Swigs the champagne.*)

MATTHEW *swipes ineffectually at* ADAM.

SHEENA/CARRIE/EDITH. Matthew!

ADAM (*recoiling, affecting an accent*). Fatty, what was that? Was that another marriage proposal?

MATTHEW *lunges again at his brother.* ADAM *dives out of the way.* MATTHEW *chases* ADAM *around the kitchen table.*

CARRIE *watches in shock, while* SHEENA *and* EDITH *attempt to intervene.*

EDITH (*cleaning manically*). Boys, boys, careful, darlings – !

ADAM (*affecting an accent*). Less pudding, Fatty, and you might run a bit faster.

SHEENA (*drinking, interrupting*). No, no, no, stop it, stop it – !

SHEENA *succeeds in coming between the two brothers.*

Please, please don't. I can't *bear* that you're fighting over me!

The brothers stagger back, catching their breath.

CARRIE (*standing, jigging around. To* SHEENA). Oh *please.* You *love* it. (*Imitating* SHEENA.) Oh, Matthew, I'm *so* sad and alone and needy / and *desperate…*

SHEENA (*drinking, interrupting*). Says the woman with her tits on fucking stilts!

CARRIE *lunges at* SHEENA – *they fight. The brothers attempt to break them apart but become embroiled in the fighting.* ADAM *trips and falls over* EDITH.

EDITH *cries out in agony and clutches her back, bringing the fighting to a halt.*

EDITH. Adam… what have you done?

ADAM (*affecting an accent*). Me…? What about Dough Boy –

EDITH. How could you let this happen!

ADAM (*affecting an accent*). How is this my fault! / I'm not the one who –

SHEENA (*to* ADAM, *drinking, interrupting*). It's always your fault: you push and push until people say things they don't mean.

EDITH. Now everything is ruined!

ADAM (*affecting, an accent*). No, no I'm not taking the blame for this. (*To* SHEENA.) I told you he had feelings for you, Clogs, I warned you – it was never about his sensitive little soul and all about his throbbing little penis. But you didn't listen, you were so flattered – this is your responsibility! (*To* MATTHEW.) You, Chubby Broccoli, *were* trying to seduce my wife. You *were* trying to sabotage my marriage, while pretending you cared so much about me, you deceitful little shit! (*To* EDITH.) And you, you geriatric junkie, Matthew is not a 'martyr' he is a two-faced slimy liar, and you have always let him get away with everything! (*Still to* EDITH.) And you're so baked out of your mind that you let your husband get away with shagging half the home counties! (*To* CARRIE.) And you… what the fuck have you been doing? He's more likely to marry me than he is you. Get your head out your fucking arse! I will not be the fall guy for a bunch alcoholic, pill-popping, compulsive-lying, sex-offending, West End Wendies! None of this is my fault – you are all to blame!

Having deflected blame onto his whole family, Rule 4 is no longer live.

SHEENA. Well done. Top marks: ten out of ten! You've succeeded in alienating everyone you love. Congratulations!

EDITH. If I've told you once, I've told you a thousand times, if you have nothing nice to say, then you can… go fuck yourselves!

EDITH hurls the turkey platter across the room.

The following title card is displayed to the audience and obscures the rules:

'ANARCHY RULES'

MATTHEW *launches himself at* ADAM.

CARRIE *lunges for* SHEENA, *shoving her across the room.*

The brothers grapple – kicking, punching, brandishing utensils as weapons.

CARRIE *holds* SHEENA *down by the hair and pours a bottle of wine all down her dress.* SHEENA *retaliates with fist full of sprouts.*

They fight with wild, cathartic abandon, EDITH *tears apart her perfect kitchen, making as much mess as possible.*

FRANCIS *delights in the drama – smiling and waving his arm as though conducting an orchestra. At the height of the chaos,* EDITH *flips the dining table over, sending food, plates and glassware crashing to the ground, rolling towards the door to the hallway…*

…where EMMA *is standing – a fourteen-year-old girl in colourful Christmas pyjamas, entering from the hallway.*

She surveys the carnage, horrified.

Emma…!

Everyone stops short. All eyes turn towards her.

The fighting couples immediately release their grip on each other.

SHEENA. Emma…!

ADAM. Emma…!

EMMA. Mummy…? Daddy…?

ADAM. Emma… Hey, munchkin…

ADAM *steps towards his child, she backs away. He looks down at himself – his clothes are torn, and he is sodden head to toe with food, drink and blood.*

SHEENA. Emma, honey, what are you doing out of bed?

EMMA. I… I wanted to come down and tell you that…
I'd like to try and climb the hill tomorrow. I know I said
I didn't want to. But I was just scared. Because if I don't
make it to the top, then it means… I'm not good enough.
So I can't be… happy. But I've been thinking… maybe
the way I try to make myself happy has gotten all twisted
and… now it's making me miserable, but I keep doing it
anyway, because I think if I stop, things will get even
worse. But maybe I do need to stop now, and just… see
what happens. So… even though I *really want* to get to
the top… I think maybe… I don't *really need* to. And so if
I don't, then it doesn't mean it'll be awful and terrible, but
just a bit upsetting. And… I can handle that… (*Beat.*)
What the fuck are you all doing?

Lights down.

Scene Seven

Thirty minutes later.

EDITH *enters and sits in a chair. She looks at the wreckage.*

MATTHEW *enters carrying his suitcase.*

MATTHEW. Mum… is Adam…?

EDITH. Upstairs. With Sheena. Where's Carrie?

MATTHEW. She's calling a taxi. She told me if I didn't leave
her alone, she'd stab me… I'm going to head off. I don't
think I can face –

EDITH (*remaining seated*). Of course, darling, I understand.
Drive carefully and let me know when you're home safe,
won't you? You'll be all right. You've got your partnership to
look forward to, haven't you? You'll be all right, won't you?

Rule 1 flickers: 'Rule 1: Matthew must sit to tell a lie'.

MATTHEW *pulls out a chair as if he is about to sit, but then decides against it.*

MATTHEW (*remaining standing*). I don't know if I will.

EDITH. Of course you will.

MATTHEW. I don't know what I feel any more.

EDITH. Just don't do anything rash. Promise me you won't do anything rash.

MATTHEW (*sitting beside his mother*). I promise.

Rule 1 is displayed to the audience: 'Rule 1: Matthew must sit to tell a lie'.

EDITH. That's my boy. You always were the reliable one. I don't know what I'd do without you.

MATTHEW (*standing*). Thanks, Mum.

EDITH. Say goodbye to Dad on your way out. Oh, and if he's fallen asleep, turn off the television.

MATTHEW *kisses his mother and makes to leave. He pauses by the door.*

MATTHEW. I love you, Mum.

EDITH. I love you, too, darling.

MATTHEW *exits.*

EDITH *continues to stare into space.*

CARRIE *enters carrying her suitcase. She fetches her purse.*

Carrie…

CARRIE. Is Matthew…?

EDITH. Gone.

CARRIE (*sitting*). I just wanted to say goodbye.

EDITH. We'll all look back on this and laugh about it some day, won't we? This whole situation will make a good joke, won't it?

Rule 2, in its original formation, flickers: 'Rule 2: Carrie must stand to tell a joke'.

CARRIE (*standing*). No. I don't think it will.

Rule 2 disappears.

(*Remaining standing.*) I knew he didn't love me. Deep down I knew. Because you know, don't you? But he always said such wonderful things to me and that was so… But now I've seen him with his family, I realise… he does exactly the same with all of you. He sees that you're unhappy and he tells you what you want to hear. You especially, I think. Maybe he's trying to compensate for Francis, or Adam, or… Anyway, whatever it is, I don't think it's good for him, or you, or me. I'm going home now. Goodbye, Edith.

CARRIE *exits.*

SHEENA *enters.*

SHEENA. Edith, my taxi will be here any minute. I just wanted to let you know that Emma is staying the night here with Adam. We've agreed that he's going to look for somewhere else to live.

ADAM *enters.*

But don't worry, I'm not planning on making life difficult for him. Every other weekend, every other Christmas, that sort of thing. Emma's our priority, we're going to do what's right by her at every step along the way.

Beat.

EDITH *stands.*

EDITH. I'm going to check on your father.

EDITH *exits.*

SHEENA *and* ADAM *look at one another.* SHEENA *lifts her suitcase and makes to leave.*

ADAM. Wait.

> SHEENA *waits, but* ADAM *still can't find the courage. And so she turns back to the exit.*

> Wait, Sheena, don't go. Please. I'm sorry.

SHEENA. They're just words.

ADAM. I can change. I can. I know I can.

SHEENA. You say that every time.

ADAM. This time is different.

SHEENA. No, it's not…

> *Rule 3 flickers: 'Rule 3: Sheena must drink to contradict'.*

> …Actually, I don't want to fight any more. I don't care any more about who's right or wrong. I just want to be happy.

SHEENA*'s rule disappears. She turns back to the door.*

ADAM. I want to be happy, too. Just tell me how. I know how to get older. I know how to get sadder. I know how to get sicker and drunker and more sarcastic. But I don't know how to get better. I don't know how to do what you're asking of me.

> SHEENA *takes the CBT Information Pack out of her bag and gives it to him.*

> *She turns back to the door.*

> All right, all right, what if I read it, what if I do it – (*Affecting an accent.*) go see a therapist and let it all out, all the dark and shameful shit that's buried deep in my gut…

> *The following rule is displayed to the audience: 'Rule 4: Adam must affect an accent to mock'.*

> (*Affecting an accent.*) …and they write it all down in their little notebook and they judge me and I pay for the pleasure of it, and, and still it doesn't change anything, still, still we can't make it work? What if I go through all of that and it doesn't make a difference?

SHEENA. I don't know. I don't have the answer.

> SHEENA *turns to exit.*

ADAM. Matthew was wrong about the part where I stopped loving you.

SHEENA *exits*.

ADAM *stands with the Information Pack a while*.

EDITH *enters carrying a plate of food*.

EDITH. Your father's fallen asleep. Why don't you have this, he wasn't hungry?

ADAM (*taking the plate, without an accent*). I'm sorry, Mum. I'm so sorry. Sheena's right, I blame everyone but myself. When the truth is… It's no one else's fault that I'm… unhappy. I need to take responsibility.

Rule 4 disappears.

EDITH. Your father will be pleased to hear it.

ADAM. Mum, I'm not sure Dad is ever going to get better.

EDITH *begins to clean up*.

Rule 5 is displayed to the audience: 'Rule 5: Edith must clean to keep calm'.

EDITH. Why don't you sit and have something to eat?

ADAM. Why don't you sit with me? We can tidy up later. Come and talk to me.

EDITH *stops tidying and approaches the table*.

EDITH. Adam…

ADAM. Yes?

EDITH (*cleaning*). Darling, please use a coaster. It's just if it dries… and it's wood.

EDITH *continues to clean*.

After a moment, ADAM *opens the CBT Information Pack at page one and starts reading*.

EDITH *cleans to the finish –*

The End.

www.nickhernbooks.co.uk

 facebook.com/nickhernbooks

 twitter.com/nickhernbooks